SOCIAL MEDIA MARKETING

LEARN HOW TO GROW YOUR SOCIAL EMPIRE

By

MARTIN JOY

COPYRIGHT@2019

Table of Contents

Copyright

INTRODUCTION

Getting your company or personal website to rank on the three major search engines (Google, Yahoo, MSN) is the quickest and most effective way to boost your sales and grow your business. Many search engine optimization (SEO) companies charge an arm-and-a-leg for ranking services, when you can do much of the work yourself for a fraction of the cost.

Marketing your business online is easier, and more importantly cheaper, than you probably realize. By using free web marketing tools and capitalizing on free social mediums you can easily drive traffic to your website and interact with your customers for no cost and very little time. Online social sites such as Facebook, Twitter, and YouTube require nothing more than a valid email account and password, and give your business free access to millions of potential customers. Social bookmarking sites such as Digg and StumbleUpon are a couple more free resources that will spread your product or message like wildfire.

Social media, also known as Web 2.0, is no longer for the kids. Don't be fooled by the flashy profiles and young founders; networking online has become the driving force behind many marketing campaigns. Social marketing is still a new strategy for many major companies, but with literally hundreds-of-millions of users from all demographics, these free platforms provide great potential. According to a recent article on Forbes.com, social media outlets allow CEO's and companies to interact with their customers daily in a highly productive way. Starbucks, for example, uses Twitter to get direct feedback from customers and update them on new products.

The majority of Web 2.0 users are between the ages of 18-34, and while MySpace still attracts the younger crowd, Facebook, Squidoo, and even LinkedIn are great for reaching the buying public in an innovative way. The best part about these free networks is that they come with built-in blog, photo, and email applications. These are the tools that make conveying your message and redirecting traffic to your site easier then ever.

There are two simple things to remember when setting up a social networking account: use keywords in your profile name, and use a catchy profile picture. Your profile picture is the first thing that customers will see when browsing the internet or considering your online 'friendship.' Your profile picture can be your logo, but in some cases it is preferable to set up an account as the company CEO, rather than as the business itself. If you are a photographer, for example, it is well worth your time to set up a Flickr profile with examples of your best work. By setting up a free account as an individual, you can blog about your work on upcoming projects, post pictures of your business convention, and interact on a more personal level. While statistics show that a certain amount of trust is already given to a social network 'friend,' that trust only enhances when the interaction is with an individual instead of a business.

Setting up a social profile, whether it be on Facebook, YouTube, or Twitter involves finding the "Sign Up" tab (or "Join" tab) usually located on the right-hand-side near the "Sign In" tab. You will be prompted to enter your email address and new password. I would suggest using your company email or setting up a free Gmail account using your business name.

When creating a profile on YouTube and Twitter, you will be instantly asked for a username. You basically have two options here: use your company name or use an optimized keyword name. Use free online tools such as Wordtracker and Google Keywords to research what names will attract more traffic. If your business name is already optimized, then you have the best of both worlds. Keep in mind that this will be how a customer finds you on these social platforms. When a user searches for new 'friends,' they will enter a keyword to find profiles. For example, if a MySpace user is searching for an Arizona Cardinal's fan, they will type in the keyword Arizona Cardinals. If you happen to have a business selling Cardinal's apparel, using this keyword is highly productive for you.

Use the free online tool CheckUserNames.com to simultaneously check multiple social networks for user name availability. From this site you can test your keyword optimized profile name, and sign up for many accounts quickly and easily.

When it's time to fill in your personal information, don't be too professional. Have some fun with it while conveying your company's message. In order to update your personal information on MySpace, you'll have to go to "Edit Profile" under the "Profile" tab near the top of your screen. From this page you will be able to change the look of your profile and add to your "About Me" section.

After creating your account, you will have to check your email to authenticate your profile. This is why you must use a valid email address. Follow the setup steps as prompted, and within a matter of minutes you have created your first social marketing site. Of course, it's definitely not advised that you simply come out and post your product all over the network. That is a great way to get blocked and rejected by every user on every platform. MySpace comes equipped with a "Spam" tab to use when you send an unwanted or commercial email. If too many of your recipients mark your email as "Spam," you run the great risk of being banned from MySpace.

Once your profiles are created and customized, it's time to get down to work. Remember, you can have an account in every social network and can optimize each one to drive traffic back to your site. The more free profiles that you have, the more opportunity you give yourself to organically rank higher on search engine report pages (SERPS). By organically, I simply mean to rank on the top three search engines without paying for it through Pay-Per-Click strategies or paid advertising.

Each Web 2.0 platform thrives under different strategies. MySpace is a great platform for "shock-and-awe." Search engine guru's still typically stay away from this free medium. However, if you're targeting a younger crowd, have a band or gaming product, this is the perfect free resource. Tools such as Pyzam will help you build your site with flair. To market your profile, use some of your email marketing skills to reach "friends."

Use a lot of art, photos and videos to convey your message. MySpace is an extremely visual medium, and you can use this to your advantage. Use banners that redirect traffic to your site. Embed links in every picture, video, and piece of artwork on your profile that will lead traffic back to your website.

In order to find your market customer, follow the "Friends" tab to "Find Friends," where you can search by age, gender, location, and even interests. Find your customer and let them know who you are without sounding like a used car salesman. Build your profile with multiple links back to your website.

Advertising on MySpace is just as easy as setting up a profile, and, though it may take a little cash, it will drive traffic to your site. Facebook advertising is built to allow you complete control of who is seeing your ad. You create it, select exactly who will see it, how much money you are willing to spend, and an advertising timeframe. Be smart about how you word your ad, what photos or logo you use, and the money you are willing to spend. Check your numbers frequently, keeping in mind that weekends will show different results than weekdays.

After you have secured "friends" on these social networks, it couldn't be easier to tell them anything and everything you want. For example, let's say you have a new product coming out, or a discounted special. By simply posting a bulletin on MySpace, writing a blog, or posting a note on Facebook, you can reach all of your customers at once. Every time you update your website in any way, you should let your customers know. This is a great way to keep things interactive and personal between you and your Web 2.0 "friends." By attaching or embedding a link back to your website, and a few bookmarking options, you are taking your social marketing to the next level.

Social mediums such as MySpace and Facebook have an amazing way of spreading photos, videos, gossip, and most of all, questioners and personality tests. By using a simple SEO strategy known as link baiting, you can drive traffic to your site. Create a simple questioner about almost anything from a users favorite things to what they had for lunch, and send it to your friends or post it on your profile. Entice your "friends" to fill out the questioner and send it to their friends, and the cycle will continue throughout the network. It may seem like a small process, but creating a small quiz or questioner will end up reaching for more people than you might imagine.

Twitter is a social network that you truly must be a part of. It's unique in the way that it allows you to consistently update your status without being too obnoxious. The whole purpose of Twitter is to literally let your "friends" know what you're doing in every second of every day. Use Twitter to inform customers of upcoming events, specials, and newly posted articles and blogs. Let customers know how you're feeling about popular news, or a company event. Don't be too professional, but send relaxed and informational messages to your "friends" on a constant basis. Embed links back to your site, or to a recent blog that you posted.

YouTube is another free social venue that is quickly becoming the SEO guru's dream, and while it may take a bit more technical knowledge, it can be your greatest free marketing tool. Filming a short video, or throwing together a quick slideshow with music, and adding a link directing people to your site, is all the work you need to do. It rarely even matters what the video is about, as long as it's entertaining and under about three minutes. You can simply use your Windows MovieMaker to edit the video, add music, a title and credits. Be sure to include a reference to your website.

How-To videos are, and will continue to be, in demand and creating one that is short and informational will do wonders for your website. Do a little research on Google Trends or Yahoo Buzz to find out what the hot topics are, and talk about them. If you're a gamble, make a controversial video (or blog). If you can get people interested and talking, you will definitely get them to your site. This will also persuade people to bookmark your video (or blog) to share the controversy with others.

The key to YouTube marketing is filling your video description with keywords and links to your website. The only way that your video will be found is through the description that you give it. Be specific to either what your video is about, or what your business is about, without sounding too much like that used car salesman. Make your description as long as you need to, as long as the link to your website is within the first few lines. These will be the first words that a viewer will see in your description. By using optimized keywords, when users search for YouTube videos via Google or YouTube itself, your video will be at the top of the list. Don't be afraid to comment on your own video, or have a friend or employee comment to get the ball rolling.

12

Post the videos you make on other video sharing sites such as MySpace and Meta Tube, and before you know it your video will rank on Google alongside your Facebook page and company website. If you have built your social profiles and video descriptions with smart links to redirect traffic, you should notice your numbers going up.

Another free Web 2.0 marketing tool is social bookmarking. Creating a profile on sites such as Digg and StumbleUpon is similar to creating your Facebook and Twitter accounts. Bookmarking sites are used to spread the word about interesting blogs, articles, and websites. For example, on Digg a user will post a story that he found interesting about Obama's stimulus package. He will "shout" it out to all of his friends, where they'll "Digg" the article and pass it to their friends. The more Digg users that see this link, the more readers this Obama article gets. The New York Times uses Digg as its number three resource to drive traffic back to its website. If you can harness the power of social bookmarking sites like Digg, you will drastically improve your traffic. This is why it is crucial that anytime you post a blog on Myspace, a video on YouTube, or an article on your personal or company website, you must add some bookmarking options for your readers.

Adding bookmarking options to your blogs involves one simple step. It's an embed code that you will place directly into your work. Check out AddThis.com to get the code and customize your bookmarking options.

SocialMarker.com is another great free resource for creating accounts on many different bookmarking platforms and easily accessing those accounts. This is a platform that will actually take you from site to site, allowing you to open an account or add your blog one by one.

An SEO strategy that has been implemented by many marketing companies is to combine RSS feeds with social bookmarking. (An RSS feed is a way of syndicating your content throughout the internet to anyone who is subscribed to receive it). Your employees should all be subscribing to your RSS feeds already. Anytime you post a new blog or article, they should be automatically notified. Their step is to choose one of the many free bookmarking sites, post your blog on that site, and thus spread the word to their Web 2.0 "friends." If each of your employees bookmarks your blog, it will appear to the search engines that you must have something relevant and important to say. Your next step is to bookmark your bookmarking profile. This will only add more relevance to your blogs and articles.

Something to consider when doing social marketing is your online reputation, and the reputation of other users. By using the free online tool Trackur.com, you can monitor yourself as well as others across many social mediums. While this product is not entirely free, it can come in handy when you need to know the atmosphere of your online network. Tweetbeep.com is a great free resource that allows you to track who is talking about you on Twitter, what they are saying, and how often they are saying it. Lastly, by using Google Alerts and setting it up manage your online reputation as well as monitoring your competitors reputation, you can stay completely informed at all times. These are great tools for staying on top of what is new in your industry, what people in your industry are talking about, what they are saying about you, and how well your social marketing strategy is going.

Social marketing is free, easy, and incredibly useful if you know how to take advantage of it. While it's still a new medium, and SEO guru's are still learning how to capitalize on it, by using these simple steps you can drive traffic to where you want it absolutely free. Take some time to do your research on keywords and effective social strategies by simply Googling social network marketing. Use the sites like MySpace, Facebook, Squidoo, and LinkedIn to get your product known. Make the most of social bookmarking sites, exploit the opportunities your own employees can offer you through their online profiles and bookmarking pages. By converging many different aspects of social media, and implementing social strategies, you will no doubt watch your sales go up. It may take a little longer to see your website rank higher on Google or Yahoo, but in time this completely free online SEO technique will work towards your advantage.

THE DIFFERENCE BETWEEN DIGITAL MARKETING AND SOCIAL MEDIA MARKETING

It utilizes an assortment of digital channels like SEO (search engine optimization), social media and PPC (pay per click) to entice audiences towards a prospective brand. Digital marketing uses internet as the core medium of promotion which can be accessed using electronic gadgets like computers, laptops, tablets and smartphones.

Internet marketing techniques such as search engine marketing (SEM), e-mails form an integral part of digital marketing. Moreover, it also includes non-internet channels like short messaging service (SMS) and multimedia messaging service (MMS), callbacks, etc. All these different channels form an integrated part of digital marketing. Digital marketing is considered a BTL Below-The-Line marketing as it targets a smaller and more concentrated group and works on forming loyal customers and creating conversions.

SMO or (SMM), on the other hand, is a branch or subset of digital marketing that excels at promotion using social media platforms like Facebook, Twitter, LinkedIn, YouTube and so forth. It makes the use of social media for the purpose of marketing. Social media relies heavily on the interaction of the users, sharing information and forming a community of sorts and hence has a 'social' element to it. It utilizes the creation of artistic content which is presented accordingly to lure the audience towards your products or services and create a brand following.

According to Zephoria Digital Marketing Consultants, there are over 1.71 billion monthly active Facebook users worldwide. This means that statistically Facebook is too big to ignore and hence, should be a vital part of your social media marketing strategies. Online video consumption on such platforms has been on a steady rise and is the next big thing in terms of marketing strategies. SMM is also a BTL Below-The-Line marketing as it relates to segregated groups formed over common interests on social media platforms.

Companies looking to address their marketing needs need to choose between a digital marketing agency or a specialist agency. If you are looking for someone to plan out your entire marketing strategy, then a digital marketing agency would be a good choice. However, if you are looking for someone to only handle the social media aspect of your strategy, then you are better off working with a specialist agency.

With the extreme popularity of digital media, people are more willing to incorporate digital marketing into their everyday lifestyle. As per the Interactive Advertising Bureau (IAB) report, Internet ad revenues in the United States reached a staggering $27.5 billion in the first half of 2015.This has opened up several job opportunities world over. There is a high demand; however, we experience a dearth in the skilled workforce as people are still coming to terms with the rapid evolution of digital media.

To meet the increasing demands of talented individuals, there are several online courses in digital marketing available. A quick Google search on this topic will enlist a host of institutes that offer the mentioned lessons. The courses run for a number of days where all the related topics under the umbrella of digital marketing are addressed. Students gain valuable insights into the subject that enables them to carve a niche for themselves.

The digital marketing course includes basic understanding of marketing and advertising concepts and fundamental knowledge of statistical and analytical tools. They are also given comprehensive information about email marketing, SEO/SEM, pay per click, mobile marketing, online video among others.

Social media marketing courses include an in-depth understanding of the principles of social media, major social media sites, social media strategy and measuring social media. It offers a look into the strengths and weaknesses of the social media platforms like Facebook, Twitter, etc. and delves deeper into the newest trends surfacing on social media.Social media is an indispensable part of digital media strategy. SM platforms are leveraged for the purpose of branding of a product or service as it provides a more interactive medium open for a two-way conversation. Digital marketing is more relevant in terms of creating brand awareness, marketing or reputation management. Although they have different online applications, they serve the larger purpose of brand advancement and customer conversion into leads and sales. Consumers have become more brand conscious with active participation and most spoilt for choice with the plethora of options available online. Their share in the overall marketing strategy has grown manifold rendering traditional strategy techniques obsolete. The rate at which digital media is advancing, it won't be far fetched to imagine a future where virtual reality has transpired to every aspect of our existence.

SOCIAL MEDIA MARKETING GUIDE FOR BEGINNERS

Social Media Marketing is the process of gaining attention and web traffic through the social media sites. During this process, usually creative content to reach the masses through publicity coming from a third-party trusted source needs to be created in order for people to share the content of their interest with others and create a vicious chain that would make business cover and go beyond the market audience intended. Every online marketer needs to have a goal, a product, a service and a cause to promote through the vast and overwhelming World Wide Web. If you already have those things defined in your mind, then congratulations! That could be probably the hardest part of entering into the social media challenge, and from now on, every single effort will contribute to reach those goals efficiently and flawlessly until you put your feet on the Social Media Guru status.

The Social Media world is wide and more extensive than ever. It is a very strategic marketing platform that reaches different cultures, ages, religion, sexes, locations, interests and such, therefore it makes it the perfect vehicle to reach and target the right audience and achieve total success. The whole world won't care about video games, for example, but only the people that video games is part of their interests. If you target male audience with ads of high heels on sale, maybe some of them would go and buy a pair or 2 for their wives, but a pair or 2 is not exactly the kind of impact you want to have. Therefore, you focus on certain group ages and certain other factors that cause some services and products, videos and news to go "viral"

First, we need to know the basic social media sites
Facebook

Holding more than 900 million users, if you're already a Facebook user this might not be really new to you, but there are lots of features worth mentioning. You can create a dedicated business page and interact directly, and free, with your customers uploading free pictures, products and videos of the service you intend to provide or the product you are trying to sell. That way, you can build a data base of people that will share your posts to their friends and therefore create the never ending chain. Most of these social media sites have seamlessly mobile integration so people whether it is a portable PC, a desktop, tablet or mobile phone get always connected with media in a way that you should take advantage of. People log in to Facebook, in any situation, while commuting, in the park, at home, at school, at work. Then you're there, promoting your business for it to be displayed in the news feeds, and you would be there, constantly doing the mind trick game to the point that people will find something attractive and worth checking according to their interests. Many big corporations like Starbucks, Microsoft, Apple, Rockstar, Pepsi etc. are doing the same, and it works perfectly!

Blogs

Blogs are an easy way for people to communicate in a semi-professional way when it comes to quality of content. Quality content is always the key to a good writing and therefore, a good blogging. There are many blogger CMS (content management service) where you can get yours up and running for free in less than 5 minutes, some of these are Blogger, WordPress and probably the most user friendly one, Tumblr. One of the tricks here is knowing your audience, your market, who you are targeting and what you want to accomplish with that. Now this has to do with some SEO or Search Engine Optimization knowledge, which is in other words, using the right keywords to rank as high as possible in a search engine i.e. Google, Bing. It has to be related to your posts and at the same time, you have to make sure you use a keyword search tool to check the competition and number of search this given keyword has. The lowest the competition and highest number of searches it gets in a month, the more convenient for you. If you were to advertise your website holding a service of technical support chat, you would have to make the keywords very specific so people that are looking for your service would find you first. It is, for example technical support for Windows, then you'll have to include specific words, as going a little more straight to the point. Since the competition would be really high and Windows technical support is a wide content, you would focus and go further the specific services your product offers, therefore, adding additional keywords to go straight to the point would be the most successful way to do it and you would rank higher in a search engine and people would find your product easily. From "Technical Support Chat" to "Technical Support Chat for Windows 7 and XP" you can see how we are narrowing the concept of the service you offer making it more specific, detailed and then competition of support for mobile operating systems, cellphones, Mac, iPhone, Windows Vista, Windows 8 and such, are left behind and those sites offering the services you're not related to won't steal your chances to be found for people that are merely looking for chat support for Windows 7 and XP. Once understood the keyword concept you can proceed and create content on a blog that would be easy to find on a search engine by including the right tags.

Then we have the Social Media integration again in the blog space. There are many options to share the content of your blog. Many Content

Manager Services like Tumblr have the social media buttons to share and like or dislike. You need to look for the options to enable them (in the rare case they are not enabled by default) so every post of yours would have the buttons for share on Tweeter, Google+, Facebook etc. and Reblog within the blogging network you are affiliated to. With great quality and eye catching content you are encouraging people to share your stories on other media sites like the ones mentioned above plus you sharing them and there you have outstanding chances to reach a wider audience.

Twitter

A fast growing, very popular social media site. With over 340,000,000 tweets a day and around 140,00,000 users worldwide, this platform is pretty appealing to business and companies as well as for celebrities, musicians, actors, everybody! A tweet is a message of 140 characters maximum that one can write and post and followers can read and see any time in their news feeds. Talk about it, interact directly and start new conversations is one of the things that make this platform extremely successful. The way they follow Kim Kardashian and read and talk about everything she tweets in a day, the same way they can do with advertising and marketing campaigns about brands and products of their interest.

140,000,000 users to target the right audience might sound like a difficult task, but seen it from the other side of the coin, that means more potential customers for a business. Once you get into the already mentioned vicious chain of any social media site, things just keep coming along by themselves and first thing you'll notice is hundreds of hundreds of people engaged in your brand, talking about it, reviewing it and telling others about events, broadcast and such.

Linkedin

Possibly a not so popular platform making it boring for some people, but a very professional and strategic one for the rest. Some people won't spend long hours chatting or talking to other about silly, trivial things, instead, this social network goes straight to the point. People on Facebook and Twitter for example, follow anyone of their interest for the sake of simply socialize as well as businesses and companies, but Linkedin is intended to filter and leave the fun behind to focus deeper in professionalism in social media.

In Linkedin, you can be part of the people looking for a job/ service, or part of a company offering a job/ service. You can create either a personal profile with your professional information about yourself, studies, contact information, interests, certifications, identifications etc. or, create a business or company page, same way as you do it on Facebook or Twitter sufficing the same purpose: share information about your brand, service, product and keep your audience and followers up to date with the latest information about your company.

YouTube

YouTube is a very interesting platform. People go watch videos of any kind or gets redirected by any website that has a backlink to it or search engines. Once people is there on a given there you have some more "Related Videos" on a column on the right side of the screen. Clicking from video to video makes you find things you never thought you would find, interesting topics, funny videos, how-to kind of videos, publicity etc. Your chances to be seen are overwhelming and you can also get people subscribe to your Channel, which is in other terms, your own YouTube space where you upload your videos. Some people find it way more interesting and easier to just watch a video rather than reading a whole article. You have the resource of visuals. If you were to promote fashion clothes and that is the purpose of your whole social media marketing, you can, along with other options, upload a video with people modeling your clothes, redirect people to your main business site, recommend people to share your video, to subscribe for future video updates, to visit your "fashion blog", like your page on Facebook, follow you on Tweeter, Google+, Linkedin, etc. Close your eyes and try to visualize the Tree Diagram of the whole Social Media marketing strategy and how it gets to potentially reach every single corner of the World Wide Web. Ambitious, isn't it?

Google+

A fairly new comer on the social media site battle, Google+ offers integration of a variety of services including Gmail, Google+ Basics, Google+ Circles that let you share information or "statuses" in a way Facebook does, but has less popularity so far. You have the "Stream" feature similar to Facebook's News Feed that would let you see what others are up to, an option for following very similar as well to Tweeter.

The service is very appealing to professionals and business networks because of the exclusivity and integration of services. You create a Gmail account for example, and unless you disable it, by default you have access to all these service and a profile ready to be edited with a picture, contact information, etc. You have access to the whole Google+ network including already mention Gmail, YouTube, You+, Circles, Basics and even the well-known search engine saving and displaying results to the most relevant things to you. It is convenient to have a spare Google+ account for any Social Media Marketer because it's potential functionality and because no source is too little or too much in marketing. Might not have the same impact, a 30 seconds ad on TV than a small billboard on a bus, but the more you get the message sent the better results you will accomplish.

Social Media Stats

According the new 87 studies perform on social media marketing up to 2012, this approach from companies to customers called B2C or Business to Community has grown and reached 16% of customer engagement but has potential to grow to 57% in the next 5 years. More than 30% of the worldwide population is now online permanently or have some sort of eventual access to the web. More than 1/5 of consumer's free time is being spent on the social media sites, reaching an approximate of 250 million tweets and 800 million Facebook statuses updated every single day. Only in the United States, more than 80% of online active users spend their on social media sites or blogs. 60% of people uses 3 or more digital forms of research product comparison, prices and information about intended purchases, being 40% of those done via social media sites like Facebook or simply redirected from one of these sites leading to even direct interactions with retailers about offers posted. Around 56% Americans have one to three profiles in a social media site being 55% of them aged between 45-55 and having at least one profile

Search Engine Optimization (SEO) facts

70% of the links search users click on are organic. 46% of all searches are for information about products or services. Half of all local searches are performed on mobile devices. 66% of new customers use search and online research to find local businesses. There are 863 million websites globally that mention "SEO." There are 9.1 million searchs conducted including the acronym each month, with the top two phrases being "SEO services" and "SEO company." More than 60,000 Twitter users include "SEO" in their bios, there have been 13 million blog posts published that include "SEO" in the title, and Amazon.com carries almost 2,700 different books about SEO 75% of searchers never scroll past the first page of results. 93% of online experiences begin with a search engine. B2B companies that maintain active content like blogging and SEO programs increased their total website traffic, on average, by 25% in the past year, while those who neglected SEO experienced an average 15% decline in overall visits. 21% of all time spent online is spent on web searches. The big three search engines Google, Bing and Yahoo! are among the five most-visited sites on the Internet. Considering that AOL is #7 and Ask is #10; five of the top 10 most-visited sites on the web are search engines.

In conclusion, Social Media Marketing is a field where professionals and amateurs in advertising can come across and put their own ideas and plans implementing their own techniques. There is no Social Media Marketer university or college degree, this knowledge that should be acquired by extensive research, it needs to be constantly employed and tested in the desired field. It is a revolutionary strategy that has taken down the old TV advertising tactics shifting it to the online market. The percentage of people that prefer to go online on a computer or capable device versus people that watches TV grows steadily every single day. Statistics show Social Media Marketing in a lower impact percentage compared to the legacy ways for advertising, but the potential it has and room for growth is in no doubt overwhelming and could be much more improved and interactive than TV has been for the past decades.

SOCIAL MEDIA MARKETING: MARKET BEYOND THE SEARCH ENGINE

The traditional technique of promoting your business in local market by distributing pamphlets, advertising on radio and television, door to door marketing are of no use now a days. The generation has changed with the change in technology every individual is now a tech savvy and want all information from internet. Since the invention of internet technology the number of users have increased tremendously, today more than millions of people are used to internet where as some totally depend on internet to earn for livelihood. In this modern generation where peoples are daily addicted to internet, it has opened a great source for promoting or advertising business online.

In the beginning when internet was new in market, no one had ever thought that it will open such a great source for generating customers to business. As the number of users increased and became great sources of attraction to people worldwide every business entrepreneur started thinking to advertise their business online. But it wasn't as simple as the technology was not so advanced the cost per advertisement online was touching sky. With the time many new sites started establishing and everyone started offering space for advertisement, at last a big change came into existence this was when the social media sites were invented.

Social media sites were those sites where people were coming for entertainment, such as for viewing or sharing video, music, etc... Social media also included sites that were giving free registration service and invited people to connect with each other for sharing their ideas. The social networking websites like Facebook, MySpace, etc were some of those sites providing free services. People didn't thought they would use these social networking sites for promoting or marketing their business. But later when the number of users started increasing and the site became famous, everyone was attracted to advertise their product and service.

The invention of Social media or social networking sites was done with the intention to share views, photos and video with the loved ones. Each and every user registered to these social networking sites wanted to raise their number of friends or fans. With the increase in number of friends they also got the royalty to be the oldest member of these social networking sites. This increased number of friends attracted many big business firms to advertise their product and services. The person with lots of friends added got huge revenue for advertising product and services of any big business firm.

Later on many companies created their own business profile in these social networking sites and started promoting their products online. With the increasing number of users the competition for advertising on these social networking sites also increased tremendously. Each and every business firm wanted to increase the number of friends and fans in their profile, but the task wasn't that easy as they thought. With the increasing competition every business firm was serious in promoting their business profile on top hence they started hiring professional social media marketers. These professional social media marketers were the oldest users of social media sites and had A to Z knowledge of social media rules and regulations.

They were capable in advertising and promoting business in social media sites very effectively, however their fees hiring these professional social media marketers were very high. But now days the numbers of social media marketers have increased and today you can find hundreds of marketers ready to take your project at cheapest rate online. If you don't have the budget to hire a professional social media marketer you can also start promoting your business yourself there are some important points that you need to keep in mind before promoting your business product or service in social media sites.

Just creating a business profile online is not enough to promote your business online you need to increase the number of fan in your profiles. Profile without friends or fans are useless for promotion, hence this is considered the important point to keep in mind before promoting your business online. Second and most important point is to provide useful product and service to the viewers; you should always check whether the product you are promoting is useful to the customer. You can judge this by practicing the product or service yourself, if you feel satisfied with the product or service than you can promote with full confidence online.

Social media marketing is considered a powerful service to provide a strong impact on your business, but before that you need to have a very strong impact our profile. If you profile looks dull and is not having attractive news or information for viewers they will not be interested in adding you to their friend list. When you register to social media sites you are not kept private all your information's are viewable by others hence you should be very attentive and serious for creating a powerful profile online. Provide something different or unique to customers online they should get to know that I am important to certain business and I should take the initiative to promote the business online.

Like this you can easily let your clients or customers carry you to the next level, when you provide special discount or voucher for your clients online this attract lots more people who are interested in getting discounted services from your business and hence they will add you to their friends or fan list. With the help of social media marketing you can generate good leads for your business, the number of visitors or traffic

34

to your website will also increase tremendously. Once you are up with a successful business profile on social media sites you will get guaranteed leads on your promotion for every single product or brand.

With the help of these social media sites you will be able to generate high leads and sale with maximum ROI in your business. Many business firms are optimizing the social media marketing strategy for promoting their business; don't waste your time because your competitor might have made the decision to promote their business online. Good Luck!

YOUTUBE FOR BUSINESS PURPOSES

If you are promoting a product or service then you simply should be using YouTube for business. This site gets millions of visitors each day and you could be attracting some of these visitors back to your website.

Use tags

If you have created a video you are happy with then load it up to YouTube. As part of the loading process you will be asked to enter what are called tags. These are basically keywords relating to your video content. When using YouTube for business, good keywords are really essential.

If your video is about an iPod for instance and someone typed these words into the YouTube search box your video may show up in the search results. Then again it may not.

By adding the tags you are giving people a better chance of finding your video. Your tags can be related to iPod so you could have tags of MP3 player, MP3, learn iPod etc. This is the way you could be using YouTube for business because with more tags you are giving people more options for locating your content.

You may be expecting people to type in the word 'iPod', but some people think differently. An iPod to you is an MP3 player to someone else

36

perhaps. This is the beauty of using tags in YouTube. You are anticipating what people are likely to type in when searching for your video content.

If your brand is well known you could use that as a tag also. There is no telling exactly what people are likely to type when searching for content either on Google or YouTube.

Another good example is the term 'Football'. In many countries it is called just that, but in the USA they know it as soccer. Someone may type in soccer when looking for football so again your tags need to reflect this.

Categorise your videos

Assign the correct category to your video also to make it easier for people to find. These are pretty important because it is the way YouTube uses to filter through the many videos that are held. There are millions there and categories will help to speed searches up.

Ensure that you have chosen the proper category for your video. If you are teaching something then assign your video to the 'how to' category. Don't worry if you feel you want to change it as you are allowed to do this at any time.

Create your own VLog

When I use YouTube for business I like to add videos to my blog. If you have done any blogging then you may have heard of video blogging. This is also known as a VLog.

After uploading a video to YouTube you have the option to mark it as VLog. This tells YouTube the playlist is a VLog in your YouTube channel. You will need to research things like channels and playlists to get a full grasp of this.

How to get more views on YouTube

The truth is, if you plan on using YouTube for business marketing, the only way you will increase YouTube views is if you create a great quality video. Sure there are services out there that will get you more views, but you should avoid these things.

You risk having your account banned if you use any underhand viewing tactics and all your videos pulled. Do you really want to take that chance? All that effort that you put in to creating your video has been wasted. Just create videos that give value and that people enjoy and you will get more views.

How to promote your product

If you offer a product or service and want to take advantage of YouTube for business, then create a video to showcase your work. You do not necessarily need to appear on screen. You can create a slide presentation which contains what you want to say. Just narrate out loud over the words on screen.

Mention the main features of the product and of course the benefits. Add photos of the product to give even more visual impact. Don't get carried away and make it a long drawn out production. Keep it simple and keep it short, around two minutes is usually enough.

People love to see visual content and you are offering good value by creating a video. When you have finished the slides then just convert them into a video file and upload it to YouTube. Add your contact details in the video as well as in the YouTube description box.

YouTube and Facebook for business

You've created that all important video masterpiece. It's up on YouTube and you are starting to see some views and visitors coming to your website. Now it is time to ramp up the traffic even more.

You may or may not have heard of Facebook. This is the biggest social networking site in the world and is now only second in terms of power, to Google. Some say it is even bigger. Only time will tell. The point I am trying to make here is that the massive subscriber base on Facebook is something you can use to your advantage. You can use both YouTube and Facebook for business by making them work together.

One thing you can do on both Facebook and YouTube is promote your video content to your friends. You will find a share button on YouTube which allows you to share your video to your Facebook account. Your friends see it and if they like it they visit your website. Now are you starting to see the potential when you use YouTube for business purposes?

On Facebook, using the share box, you can directly type the URL of your YouTube video and share it that way also. This is a unique way of using YouTube for marketing purposes.

Why not create a Facebook fan page showcasing your company or product. You can bring into it any YouTube videos you have created. Now you are opening it up to the whole of Facebook and your audience is widening.

Conclusion

If you use YouTube for business purposes, you have to use a bit of imagination to get your content viewed. It opens up a whole new world of marketing to you.

YOUTUBE TRAFFIC FOR BUSINESS

Over the past few years it is safe to say that online video has literally exploded. The growth of video has led to business worldwide to see the potential of a new video marketing strategy. The best video traffic is experienced from YouTube traffic; there is no doubt about that.

YouTube has experienced massive growth since its inception. An example of the growth can be found in a recent statistic which stated that roughly 48 hours of video content is uploaded to the site every minute. I'm sure you will agree this is nothing short of amazing.

There are other video sites around and they are indeed worth uploading your video to. However, the traffic you get from these is nothing compared to what you can expect from YouTube traffic. If people like your product or even your video then there is a good chance they will come and visit your website to find out more about you.

It does not matter if you want to watch the latest movie trailers, music videos or just 'how to' videos. You will find it all on YouTube. If you have a business, product or service, here are some ways your business can benefit from YouTube traffic.

Mass exposure

No other video site can command the same type of worldwide audience as YouTube. This is the site we all head to when we need to check out a video. Now think how such a massive user base can be beneficial for your business.

Create your own channel

YouTube allows you to create what are known as channels. This is essentially your own personal space for holding your videos. You can customise the channel how you want. When all your videos are in one place under a channel it makes them easier to locate and in turn will get you even better YouTube traffic.

As more and more people like your channel content they will add it to their favourites. You may also add the channel in your own blog or website.

Build your subscriber list

Perhaps you have an opt-in box on your website that collects names and email addresses. You can now add video to your opt-in box to create a more visual interactive feel. I can think of one famous marketer in the dating niche who increased his conversions overnight when he embedded video into his opt-in area.

To get a flood of YouTube traffic you can use YouTube to host your video and then all you need to do is add it to your opt-in page.

Professional image

Having video on your blog or website conveys a more professional image. Standard text is fine, but video enhances the page even more. The user may see your video on your site or on YouTube, but either way you appear more authentic by having video.

Explode your traffic

YouTube being the global site it is means YouTube traffic is flowing day and night. Because the world is divided into time zones it means while you are asleep in say London, someone in Australia, where it is now morning, could be watching your video.

You do not need to upload just one video. As mentioned above, why not create your own channel and add as many videos as you want there. The more you add the better YouTube traffic rank you are likely to get.

Search engine optimization

YouTube is owned by Google. Having two massive internet sites under one umbrella represents fantastic possibilities for your business.

Google loves video content and if you have it on YouTube they will love you even more. Your website page will be nicely optimised for the search engines if it has YouTube video content.

Now Google shows both text and video in the search results. What if your video is returned when someone is searching? Think what this could mean for your sales and potential YouTube traffic that could be coming to your website.

You can increase YouTube traffic by building backlinks to your videos. Also make sure you bookmark your videos.

Video articles

If you have written any articles and submitted them to article sites then you know how valuable this can be. People love to read articles and come to the article sites to do just that.

When an article is syndicated it is spread virally across many sites and you get some nice traffic. Imagine if you could do the same with video and get YouTube traffic along the way. Well you now can in the form of a video article.

A video article will contain the most important parts of your text article. A camera is not needed to make this kind of production. You just need the correct software and a little imagination.

You can convert your text article into on screen text that the viewer can read in the video. You then speak out loud the words. It is worth adding other material such as photos to vary it up a little.

A well-made, two minute video article can offer great value to people and get you some phenomenal YouTube traffic.

I recently created a short production on how to combat stress. I added text to slides and also brought in photos for things like meditation. I also added some music to give the production more of a professional feel.

The traffic you can get from video articles is as good as any standard video. By hearing an actual voice people are immediately starting to trust you and are happy to visit your website. You may choose to use YouTube traffic statistics to monitor any traffic you are getting.

Video articles will do wonders as part of any YouTube promotion you use in your business.

You must be careful to use copyright free music as YouTube have strict guidelines on what you should use. I know you see a lot of videos on there with music you recognise, but in time those videos may be removed. All the YouTube traffic you have built up is gone in the process. A quick Google search should lead you to some sites which offer royalty free music to use.

A good free music editing tool to use is something called 'Audacity'. This will allow you to edit your music so that it fits the length of the video. You can also add effects such as fading etc to the music. You will find 'Audacity' by doing a quick search on the internet.

If all this is beyond you then outsource it to someone who can create video, edit music etc. They will also be able to upload it to YouTube and optimise it for the search engines.

Conclusion

By getting more and more YouTube traffic you are getting mass exposure for your products which can only be good in the longer term.

Having video to promote your business should be how you focus your marketing strategy. You will reap the rewards in both subscribers and sales.

YOUR INTERNET MARKETING BUSINESS AND YOUTUBE

Search Engine Optimization is a big concern for internet marketers. It is a vital key to increasing the popularity of an online business. Being in the internet marketing industry, you are probably very aware by now that a well optimized site also equates to bigger income.

I have met several internet marketers who are seeking techniques on how they can further optimize their sites. Are you also looking for more ways on how you could further make your internet marketing business progress?

Indeed, there are various ways which you could use. For now, let us focus on one technique which can be truly effective in optimizing your online business. That is, video marketing through YouTube.

If you are thinking that up until today, YouTube is merely a venue to share videos and highlights of people's daily lives, then you have to take a closer look at that venue. YouTube has also evolved as a great tool for online businesses. Other internet marketers think that it is difficult to use this site for internet marketing. Actually, it can require some extra effort in creating the videos but once you get the hang of it, you will see that it is not really as difficult as you first thought it would be.

48

Apart from contributing to the progress of your online business, YouTube also has a lot of benefits. First of all, using YouTube for your internet marketing business does not entail fees. You can upload your videos and allow the entire world to see it without having to worry about paying monthly fees. It is a free service. It also works around the concept of tags and keywords so you will also be able to apply your prior knowledge about search engine optimization if you decide to venture into video marketing through YouTube.

I would like to share with you some helpful tips on how you can really use YouTube for your internet marketing business. Hopefully, this can make things much easier for you.

1. Conceptualize well for your video. I have seen other internet marketers who skip on the conceptualization part. They just go right on creating videos and uploading it instantly on YouTube with the intention of making it contribute to the progress of their online businesses. Then, they would realize after some time that their video does not exactly deliver what it is supposed to. That is because, they end up creating a video which fails to capture the interest of the viewers. The best way to go is to strategize well before jumping into shooting and making your

video. Think of what topic you should discuss and how this will cater to the people that you are targeting for. It is important to make it unique and interesting to watch. You may want to create a draft of the things that you would like to say on the video and the images that you would like to incorporate in it. This way, the entire process will not only be much easier, you would also be able to come up with one that encapsulates your credibility and knowledge. Remember, it also has to be informative so that more people will pay attention to your videos and will end up being your customers too.

2. Exude professionalism. The main reason why some people look for videos to watch on YouTube is because they are seeking more knowledge and information. If you want people to become interested in your online business it is vital for you to let them know that you are a professional. Make them aware that when it comes to the products that you are offering and the niche that you chose for your business, you are knowledgeable and that you can really provide solutions to their concerns. It can be a good approach to be a bit casual since this will enable you to establish relationship with the viewers. Just remember that

you have to maintain good quality in the videos that you will make. Check clarity of audio and video before you upload your videos in YouTube. With professionally done videos, you will also be able to gain their trust and confidence in you.

3. Maximize the potential of your videos by using the title, description and tags well. Do not think that the title is not important because you have relevant information in your video. Titles play a big role when it comes to the number of views that your YouTube videos will get. For viewers, they look into the title even before they open the video. So, it is important to make it catchy. It should also sum up what your video contains. This way, more people will become interested and actually go on watching it. Also, make your videos easier to be located with the proper usage of tags and descriptions. Tag you videos with relevant keywords. Come up with an interesting and concise summary too.

4. Always check and double check. It is not enough to just check everything one time. Make sure that you will double check you videos before you upload it. Once you have already uploaded it on YouTube, double check so you can make sure that everything is working properly. Try watching the video and see if it loads up easily and if there are no

technical problems with it. This way, you can make sure that the other people who will view your video will not encounter any problems which will make them lose interest.

5. Create backlinks to your videos. The main purpose of the videos you will create and post in YouTube is for you to increase the optimization of your internet marketing business. What you could do is post your videos on the social networking sites which you also use for your online business. You can also embed the videos on your website so it will also be easily accessible through it.

While you are making your video which you intend to upload on YouTube, just keep your goals in mind. Since your main purpose is to promote your website for better search engine optimization, incorporate it within the video so the viewers will easily be able to locate your website.

Hopefully, these few tips will help you in your video marketing through YouTube.

YOUTUBE MARKETING-HOW TO GET MORE VIEWS ON YOUTUBE

Knowing how to get more views on YouTube is critical. If you don't have the views, your competitors get them. There are hundreds of ways to get more views on YouTube, however some of them require a team of people or outsourcers or specialized and expensive software and are not feasible for a small business. There are some very easy ways to get more views on YouTube videos that anybody can implement which is what we will talk about here.

Easy Ways To Get More Views On YouTube Videos

Now, to get more views on YouTube videos, there are some basics that everyone should do. One thing that is always good to do before you even make a video is to go "spying". Check up on the people who will be your direct competition and see what they are doing. What have they titled their videos and what sort of phrases are they targeting? What is in their description and what do they link to? Do they have their own channel? Do they interact with comments or do they even have the comments turned on?

All of these things will give you some clues about how easy it is going to be for you to compete with them. If you already have your video setup and online, let's tackle some of the easiest ways to get more views on YouTube videos that you already have.

1. Share Your Video With Everyone. If your video is something that a wide range of people will be interested in, start sharing it everywhere. Every time you talk to somebody, mention it, put it in your signature and get everyone on your social media accounts to check it out. This is obviously basic stuff, but it's how you get the ball rolling and get from 5 views up to 500 or 1000.

2. Comment On Other Videos. Every time you watch a video, comment on it. Don't spam it with stupid comments but offer them your thoughts or critiques and some help. Then you can leave a link back to your video. Hint: the better your comment, the more likely it will end up in the top comments section and your link will stay there! This doesn't mean you only get more views on YouTube, but also on Vimeo and other video hosting sites. Even when you are just reading a blog post or a forum, leave a link back to your video if it is appropriate.

3. Get More YouTube Friends. Seek to create friendships with as many people as possible and then start to network with them, you can create networks of people that share each other's videos and this can be a powerful way to spread the love. Don't reach out to direct competitors and hope that they will mention your video, instead reach out to people who are in sub niches or side niches. If you want to get more views on YouTube channels about making muffins, try to find people who make cheesecakes.

4. You won't be stealing each other's customers but instead helping each other out as you are serving slightly different markets. Don't overdo this though, if you add thousands of people at once you will get a stern warning from YouTube. Get more views on YouTube by being a real person and slowly add a certain amount of friends each day. View it is a long term plan instead of spending one day adding 2500 friends and hoping they view your channel.

5. Promote Off YouTube. You can get more views on YouTube by promoting your videos in hundreds of places online, but there are certain places that are far more likely to attract the people you want. If you have a video about how to Zumba, go and find

some blogs about Zumba dance that are semi popular, read the post and leave a link back to your video. This highly targeted way of getting more YouTube views works because you are focusing only on people who are already interested. Find forums about Zumba-ing or other types of workout dance classes, and you will have thousands of people who are interested in your video, but would have otherwise not found it.

6. Get More Views On YouTube With Social Bookmarking. If you have a video about how to clean a DVD player, create accounts at popular social bookmarking sites such as StumbleUpon, Twitter, Pinterest, Digg and Diigo and add them there. These will help you get views and a few backlinks to your video to help push it up the rankings a bit. Getting backlinks from these sites and the previously mentioned blog comments, forum postings and links on other YouTube videos all helps to send the message that your video is getting more popular. Don't forget to tag your videos and give them a good title when submitting to these sites. There are plenty of free tools to do mass social bookmarking online, however you still need to create an account with each site you wish to use.

Where Do You Start?

With all of these options it can be a headache just wondering where to start. Just picking one simple thing and doing a little bit each day toward the process will get you started in the best way. Trying to do too many of the steps will not get you more views on YouTube because you will give up. Just pick one method to focus on and you will get more views as time goes by because you are slowly building up the links to your content.

Before you try all of these methods above, it is highly recommended that you ensure you have all of your basic video properties are up to par. Make sure your video is titled and capitalized as necessary, tagged properly and has a good start image. Make sure that you don't overload your video with too many annotations, instead have one pop up just for a few seconds a couple of times during the video to encourage people to view more videos, subscribe or other action you desire. If you can do this you will get more views on YouTube easily, but it is a process and not something you can just do overnight.

IDEAS FOR IMPROVING SEO ON YOUTUBE

It is not a surprise to keep in mind the enhancing appeal of YouTube as a vibrant and a favored marketing platform over other more developed social networks websites like Facebook, Twitter as well as Google. The flexible marketing functions of YouTube by means of videos have actually improved lots of online company websites internet search engine rankings as video marketing delights in a higher degree of receptivity in the market over other internet marketing strategies.

YouTube appears to be an extremely preferred marketing platform compared with other social networks platforms with more web users plying its platform daily for interesting and brand-new videos to promote their senses and amuse themselves.

Entrepreneur and online marketers are looking for to improve SEO on YouTube with a greater ROI that would benefit their brands and company profits.

1) Developing a Strong Market Presence

Company owner and online marketers need to work vigilantly in developing a strong market presence of their brand and company throughout the board on all platforms that hold the capacities in marketing themselves to draw the specific niche markets. YouTube is an enhancing favorite on marketing platforms today to draw natural traffic to the sites.

A strong market presence on YouTube consists of an excellent branding of business and site with white hat SEO includes well engaged. When business shows a clear exposure in the market, it would be considered a market leader or material professional in a certain specific niche that would draw in the ideal audience to its site for more revenues and sales.

This large market exposure on YouTube would be produced through high quality and vibrant promotion videos which are helpful and amusing to targeted audiences. Well produced discount videos are most likely to stir beneficial customer feelings to the brand and company that would stimulate off the ideal call-to-action choices by the customer to business.

2) Wise Application of Competitive Keywords

Excellent video searches on YouTube still need the very best of competitive keywords or expressions that would have the ideal audiences visiting rapidly and often. Well produced videos integrate the most recent vibrant SEO functions that impart the best keywords that allow quick and effective online searches.

Web company owner and online marketers who prepare to control YouTube marketing by means of amusing promotion videos might take advantage of on Google's keyword organizer device that assists YouTube users discover the best keywords to their favored videos rapidly. This would enable the usage of long-tail keywords that would have an online video search to be more particularly recognized for a quicker search.

Competitive keywords need to describe those which targeted users would type in to discover the desired brand or company video. Such keywords have to be included rightly in the video title or description that would assist users discover exactly what they desire; which is business video that has actually placed the ideal keywords tactically by means of SEO choices.

3) Exceptional Video Descriptions

A vibrant title to draw in the ideal audiences to the discount video, the description of the video is similarly crucial in improving more views and prospective company leads. The apt deployment of excellent video thumbnails serves to direct audiences and prospective company clients to the video.

If it were seen, an apt video description would likewise encourage audiences on their option of videos by comprehending the advantages of the video. An exact and clear description of the video contents would assist possible audiences pick the video for a complete viewing.

An ingenious video description would have the ability to engage prospective audiences to have a clearer mind prior to seeing; this is extremely advantageous to enhancing brand understanding as the video is viewed. The right and succinct description of the description column is part and parcel of excellent SEO that might create much better traffic to the web company website by means of the video.

The video description serves to promote branding the company appropriately to accomplish the set objectives on SEO through YouTube.

4) Viral Video Marketing

In order to increase SEO on YouTube, entrepreneur and online marketers need to discover how to control the very best in digital marketing and the most recent innovations that would add the wanted results in every marketing method and project. This would indicate a desire to produce a vibrant discount video on business brand and operations that might trigger the video on YouTube to go viral.

A viral video is the very best marketing ad a company might expect today as this would trigger enormous natural traffic to come along. A viral video is a strong indicator of marketing success that might be transformed into company success with greater earnings and sales, specifically if business owners or online marketers are prepared to deal with the result. In order to produce a vibrant video that would go viral on YouTube, the video manufacturer need to comprehend the goal of the video and the readily available devices to be engaged to trigger the viral impact.

This might consist of factors to consider on existing market patterns, most current customer habits and needs, video contents and title in addition to the quality and effect of the video on audiences.

5) Right Marketing Characteristics

With the best deployment of vibrant marketing techniques on producing a flexible discount company video on YouTube, the ideal SEO functions need to be integrated from start to complete for the very best of SEO in the video on YouTube.

When the best actions are taken in enhancing SEO on YouTube, it is most likely that the preferred outcomes would drop by in a matter of days. Company owners and online marketers have to team up carefully with video manufacturers to engage the ideal SEO aspects that would produce the wanted high quality appealing video which increases business and branding.

Imaginative videos on YouTube might be on any subject in various methods to win over target market making use of quality material and discussion while promoting the brand and company. Fantastic video functions with SEO need to be included to have actually interested audiences directed to the site to be decided in on business subscriber list as opt-in customers.

Conclusion

Excellent quality and ingenious YouTube videos bring in a greater viewership with a capacity of the video going viral and improving SEO at the exact same time.

YOUTUBE INFLUENCER MARKETING MISTAKES TO AVOID

We can say, YouTube Influencer Marketing is one of the best ways to increase a Brand's reach. But, if and only if we do it the right way.

In 2016, there are up to 75% of marketers are now investing in influencer marketing, 60% of brands will increase the amount they spend on influencer marketing. However, the recent research shows that YouTube has the best ROI than any other social media platform, knowing that YouTube is the second largest search engine and it has the monthly user base of more than 1 Billion users. Impressive, right? It's no surprise that YouTube sponsorships are one of the present's top-ranked customer acquisition tool.

YouTube Marketing could offer you huge rewards. However, the way to reach the success from its uncharted territory can be bumpy. Here are top marketing mistakes that are often encountered and strategies on how to avoid them:

Goals Without Strategy. This is one of the common mistakes a marketer makes when launching YouTube Influencer Campaigns. They only focus on their goals and objectives. Some marketers focus on achieving a goal of a certain amount of views and interactions, specifically

64

likes, comments and shares per video they conduct across several channels.

An ROI positive YouTube Influencer campaign requires a well-analyzed strategy. Aside from numeric campaign goals, a marketer should consider defining KPIs or key metrics which indicates whether a campaign's performance can achieve the set goals. In this case, this will allow for better decisions and strategies not just to meet the ultimate objectives, but to reach the goal higher than the expected.

Discovery. This is a crucial stage that will define the campaign's success. In this stage, marketers often fell into a very common trap which is choosing a talent based on the channel's number of subscribers and latest video views.

YouTube hosts much larger amount of data on video watching. The increase of Big Data analytics could provide online tools to help themarketers dig deeper to find the highest-quality talent for their brand. Several key data-driven aspects should analyze when choosing a talent. These are:

- Relevance. Is determined by keywords and audience overlap. Which also identifies whether a channel's audiences will be authentically interested in your service or product.

- Reach. The average number of view per video. It is calculated as the average number of views during a set period of time.

- Engagement. It is usually computed using total views and interactions. It measures how actively the audience interacts with the channel's content.

- Influence. It is calculated based on how content is shared on the channel and if viewers are turned into subscribers. It also indicated whether a channel stimulates action and audience growth.

- Consistency. It is measured by averaging various channel performance metrics from video to video. It analyzes how often the channel is delivering meaningful content.

If a marketer fails to analyze any of these crucial parameters, the campaign may result in a poorly targeted audience, low conversion rates, and washed budgets.

Popularity. Any industry has its most popular YouTube celebrities with millions of subscribers. It seems like the fastest and easiest solution for a brand, but remember, they only represent 1-5% of all influencers.

Hundreds of new channels are created and published every day and marketers are playing it safe, they activate the largest channels to secure the best results and keep on ignoring smaller channels. This may lead to disappointment, there are more opportunities from smaller channels. This strategy provides only mediocre outcomes. Why?

- Lack of Authentic Admiration. There is a lot of things going on for the most popular influencer. They cover a variety of topics, experimenting with different video ideas, in fact, they often treat brand partnerships as just another business, Isn't it true? They also spend a big amount of time on marketing. The result it: Those brands do not get any special interest or authentic excitement about their product or service. Smaller and niche channels are sincerely interested in the particular topic and products, which could lead to higher quality endorsements.

- Lack of Targeting. For example, when a channel has a large scattered audience, it's difficult to predict which portion of subscribers would actually be interested in the particular brand and/or topic. This may result in subscribers can see videos that are irrelevant to their interests, which could hurt both the influencer and the brand. However, small and mid-sized dedicated channels attract a homogenous audience of highly engaged followers.?

Marketers must explore the small and middle-sized niche channels, which can become the most loyal and dedicated brand ambassadors that open doors to a highly targeted and engaged audience. More or less amount of marketing dollars, brands can reach a greater variety of audiences and produces multiple pieces of content.

Losing Control. Marketers still fall into the trap of treating an influence as an actor and editorial content as video ads. The Brands underestimates how keen their users are, how fragile their trusts are and how shortsighted it is to fake authenticity.

Case Studies prove that the more authentic the content is, the better users react to it. This leads to higher reach, better engagement and ultimately, stronger campaign results.

Agency. As the number of YouTube influencers arise, agencies also rise to help brands with campaigns. Marketers can fully outsource the efforts and simply reap the rewards. But there are a lot of pitfalls hidden in this strategy.

- Limited Access. The agency only has the access to talent in its network, those channels may not always be the best fit for the brand's needs. Marketers should not fail to assess channel's value and not to limit their reach to only one ideal partner.
- Connection. Lack of connection is what marketers often underestimate, especially the level of personal connection which

is required for a brand and an influencer. Influencers do seek strong relationships and connection with a brand so they could truly understand its values and speak on its behalf.

- Niche Understanding. The majority of agencies cater to brands within multiple industries and don't fully understand the subtle differences of particular spaces. The brand manager should step in and make sure that both talent and video content choices are taken to consideration industry specific aspects.?

In working with agencies, managers need to carefully evaluate the emerging costs compared to the delivered value, the differences between the overhead associated with launching campaign in-house and the agency fees, the key competencies and resources the team is missing and if they are provided for by the partner. Managers need to find out answers to these variables before hiring an agency.

Lack of Transparency and Standardization in Pricing Models. This is one of the biggest challenges for marketers in YouTube Influencer marketing. Marketers end up getting unreasonably high quotes and overspend. Not realizing the room for negotiation in the market.

- Payment Models. Different channels and agencies work on different payment models like pay per view, pay per action and/or pay per activation. Most of agencies or talents work solely on pay per activation model and often do not tie their fees to guaranteed campaign results.

- Marketplace. YouTube influencer marketing is still in its infancy, with a lack of benchmarks, the market has not determined average rates. Influencers and agencies currently charge anywhere from $0.02 to $0.20 per view so there is a lot of room for negotiation.

Secret Transactions. Agencies share their pricing structures rarely which lead to partners offering different fees for the same talent or campaign. Marketers are required to compare prices across space and negotiate aggressively to get the best deal, this will secure an ROI positive campaign.

YouTube Influencer Marketing is one of the excellent ways to expand your reach. Execute an authentic campaign with the right YouTube Influencer and you don't make costly mistakes. You can do your own research and likely have much better results.

POSITIVE AFFIRMATIONS USING YOUTUBE

Internet marketing calls for understanding the mind, with respect to it's surrounding environment. There is no need for diabolical, sneaky or tricky behavior. Consider these positive affirmations using YouTube. Advertising can be challenging and deserves respect. The concept of supply and demand is relevant, to YouTube marketing. Simply understand what you are selling and find a match, with a prospect's desire. Doing that was quite a task, before the Internet developed. People would sail the seven seas. Marketers would fly around the world. There are still sales people traveling for sales. Why would they travel? It's probably because they haven't come to a total understanding of web power.

Personal contact is ultimately a powerful sales tactic, with limits. How many people can you personally contact in a given day? There may be the expense of plane tickets, hotel bills, meals etc. Marketers use the Internet for easily making new contacts. Expenses are minimized using the Internet. You can discreetly make personal contact after your web connection. YouTube is an excellent platform for meeting people. The video element can give a detailed description of people and things.

You may analyze all you want. Nothing beats seeing things, with your own eyes. The saying pictures speak a thousand words is quite relevant here. Radio, paper media, even telephone communication is great, but I applaud and truly admire video.

Video communication is seriously appreciated, after living through the age of Xerox and telephones. Today's youth may not thoroughly understand the incredible value of web promotion. I remember beepers and message boards. That was before Windows 95. Many of you assume video sharing was always here. The changing of industry and technology has an effect upon the human psyche. I can also say the changing of the human psyche has an effect upon technology. That makes an industry change.The days of putting up a sign and selling lemonade have past, although there are some still trying to do just that.

Tradition can impede progress. I relate to a typical brick and mortar store. I'm referring to your pizza parlor. I like pizza in the morning and there are probably a lot of other folk who have the same taste. The pizza store owner would achieve morning profits, if he or she went beyond tradition. Supply and demand is a common relationship and tradition creates limits upon its progress. Many of us are too caught up in tradition. Some are not in the business at the correct time of day. That's sad and also ridiculous. An Internet store usually stays open twenty-four hours per day. The so-called pizza store can't do that. The impeding issue may be the cost of operation. A classic pizza man figures the cost of having hot pizza available 24 hrs daily is disproportionate, to the amount of customers rendering profit. You'll need an employee, unless you install a vending machine. The guy at Seven Eleven has their store open day, night and sells a variety of things. The idea here is each hour brings a different type of customer. There are many ways you can look at making sales.

Connected to a sales link is comparable to a worldwide vending machine. You can do a video to attract who ever. Make them thirsty, hungry or what have you. Then direct them to your solution. Your solution is your point of sale. It's that simple. Doing one video may be enough for perhaps Soulja Boy or Lady GaGa. You'll probably need to do several videos accompanied by a considerable amount of promotion, in order to generate income. Promoting your video can be free. The only cost is time and energy; this is where your mind can play a major role once again, for the advancement of your financial freedom. Remember for every piece of quality content you submit to the web, you will be rewarded by its presence one way or another. The more content you submit, the more recognition you get. I spoke of 3rd party recognition in my other writing and I will speak of it again here. People can see you clearly via search engine. It's common for a person to submit a keyword or phrase into the search engine, to get a response. This is how people find things. You connect with these people upon being seen in the search engine. How do you get seen in the search engine is a marketer's quest. Here is how to accomplish being seen without spending money. Use 3rd party endorsement. This is a simple concept. Who can be used as your 3rd party endorser? The answer to this question is the subject of college courses. Find viable solutions and you have free publicity.

Selling your products or services via YouTube is what others may want to do as well. You have the option to create your own affiliate program. ClickBank creates the mechanism for your own affiliate program. They will give you a unique coded link. Use YouTube, to attract people to your unique ClickBank link. You'll see other videos on your page as others will see your videos on their page. Give your affiliates examples, to promote their link. You may want to create banners and sequenced email messages. You can actually do as I'm doing now. Give article-marketing instructions. Having an army of marketers selling your product

74

or service is a wonderful thing. The commission you offer is what you determine. You can afford to give your affiliates a great commission and still make out well. ClickBank actually does the math for you. All you have to do is tell them what percent you want to give your affiliates or you can choose a set amount of the sales. ClickBank also deals with charge backs. That's why I like ClickBank as they are a full service affiliate broker working honestly. They benefit both sides of their transactions. YouTube can work in conjunction with affiliate programs like ClickBank. This is what I call a profitable blend.

Positive affirmations using YouTube include the Partner program. You may already know that you must have at least a few hundred thousand channel views, in order to get reasonable payment. It works out that YouTube pays roughly pennies on each hundred channel views. This means you must create an interesting channel. There are so many directions you can go. It may interest you that the most popular channels are basically nonsense. You have Ray William Johnson on top, at the time of this writing. He's doing a mad take off on Howard Stern, although Ray started out looking like some crazy kid ranting. I don't know what to think anymore about what people like. The rationale is usually madness. This does not mean you have to be mad in order for people to like you. It would behoove you to take a look at what is trending on YouTube, so that you can get a feel for what you are embarking upon. No matter what you do, you will need production skills. You can actually begin as an armature and develop. You don't need a camera. You can use slide shows with a free Windows program entitled "Movie Maker." You can, of course make standard video. Standing in front of a camera and talking usually works.

YOUTUBE PROMOTION

We can use YouTube for watching video clips or even whole movies now. We can also create something called 'Infomercials' and load them onto YouTube. These can be used as a YouTube promotion marketing strategy for your product or service.

But first let's look at how YouTube currently stands in the online world. Recently YouTube, which was bought by Google for $1.65 billion in 2006, was said to be streaming 4 billion online videos every day. In early 2012 this was seen as a 25% increase in the past eight months.

This increase comes at a good time because more and more people are watching video on their televisions and smartphones. Google is pushing this new way of viewing by providing great content.

YouTube figures show that around 60 hours of video is uploaded to the site every minute. That is an incredible statistic, unimaginable a few years ago and one you can exploit with YouTube promotion of your products. YouTube streams around 4 billion videos globally a day, but only around 3 billion of them are actually monetised each week.

Video checklist

It is easy to be sceptical about anything and I understand if you may be wondering does YouTube promotion work? The truth is it does, but you need to create a video that has great content first.

Before creating a video of any kind you need to have some kind of action plan or a video checklist. Do you know what your subject material is? If you intend to speak or narrate then you will need some kind of script at hand, unless you are totally confident of making it up as you go along.

One thing you do not want to happen in your YouTube video promotion is to pause when you don't know what to say next or even mumble your way through the whole production.

Plan out what you intend to say and rehearse it prior to actually recording. Try to speak clearly and confidently. You want to come across as someone knowledgeable about the subject material you are conveying.

Shoot a few rehearsal videos and watch it back. Are you happy with your vocal tone and clarity? Is there any background noise? You don't want noise from traffic or worse still, the camera motor. If you can get a second opinion then do that before shooting the actual video.

Creating the video

Now it is time to get going on your YouTube video promotion work and get your video camera ready. for the actual filming. If you do not have one of these then does your phone take good video?

If you want to show yourself to viewers then you will need a video camera of some kind. Look at all your options and test out all of them. You may find your humble phone gives you the results you need. As you make more sales you can invest in better equipment.

If you do not have a video camera of any kind for YouTube promotion then all you would need to do is incorporate photos of the product within the video itself. Create a slideshow using PowerPoint or a similar tool, bring the photos into it and then narrate your text. Talk about any benefits and features that the product has.

You will find examples of infomercials on the web. If you need to know how content should look then do a quick Google search for infomercials. Also search for video podcasts.

Add a title in your infomercials and start off with a cheerful greeting. A good intro is important in your YouTube promotion strategy as this is what will hook the viewer in initially.

Try to end the video well also. You need to thank people for taking the time to watch your video. Add a call to action and provide your website link so that people know how to contact you. Packages such as Windows Movie Maker are free and can create some nice titles and animation for your video.

Of course the most important part of the video is the actual body. This is where you will engage the viewer and keep them watching. You have to make it good otherwise the viewer may click elsewhere.

Try not to sound boring in the video and keep the length to two minutes. Engage the viewer and speak with a clear voice at all times. Bu doing this you will be well on your way to having a YouTube promotion video to be proud of.

If someone likes your video they could turn into a customer. You want people to click back to your website to see what products or services you can offer them.

Ensure that you talk about what your product can do for them and how it is going to solve their pressing problems.

You can use Infomercials nicely for tutorial videos also. Why not put them onto your blog and use YouTube promotion to emphasise what people are going to gain from your tutorials. Make a quick clip of your tutorial and insert your website link to tempt them.

For anyone looking for a job, you will find creating an infomercial that promotes you is going to be very beneficial. Mention your skills, experience and qualifications. What this is in effect is, is a video resume and you can also state what kind of job you would like. The potential here for YouTube promotion is enormous.

YouTube marketing

When you are happy with the final video it is time to put it somewhere where people can access it. The best place in my opinion is YouTube for two reasons.

Firstly because it gets billions of viewers globally each day, it can only be of benefit to you. Imagine the amount of YouTube traffic you could be getting as a result of many people watching your video. This represents great exposure for your product, service or business.

Secondly, you want to keep YouTube promotion costs low, or as low as you can. So what is the YouTube promotion cost you may be asking yourself? The great thing about YouTube is that it is free to upload and host your video. Yes the beauty is that your videos are getting free YouTube promotion and exposure.

If you are intending to add more than one video onto YouTube then it is worth setting up your own channel. This will allow you to centralise your videos and brand yourself. You can customise the look of your channel if you so wish to help with any YouTube promotion, although this is not necessary.

Before you upload your video ensure that the name you give to the video file has your chosen keyword somewhere in it. Also add your keyword to the title and description once it is uploaded. This helps to optimise the video for the search engines and enables people to find it.

Conclusion

Your business, whether large or small, needs YouTube promotion as part of its marketing strategy. The more people that watch your video the more likely you are to make sales. Add video to your marketing today and see how it can benefit you.

ADVERTISING ON YOUTUBE

In comparison to advertising online across other mediums such as Facebook or using Google AdWords to reach people on a CPC (cost per Click) bid basis where clicks can become more expensive due to the bidding process, advertising on YouTube is a very economical way to get the word out about your products or services. For only about 2-3 cents a click, you are in business with people viewing your ads.

There are some challenges with advertising through this medium however. The first of which is that you often will have to create a video advertisement as opposed to just an image you post with a clickable component that allows the viewer to learn more about the product and purchase it. Video advertising means you have to get more creative and that can be a barrier for some but it really does not have to be as difficult as you might think.

For example, when people traditionally think of creating videos, they think of capturing movement and action - just like you would see on a TV advertisement or in a movie. This is an expensive and time consuming way to create an ad but you really don't have to be that elaborate if you don't want to. To explain, you can also create ads using tools like Microsoft PowerPoint or even just using.jpg images. What you do is find or create slides or images you would like people to see, put them in a sequence using a video editing tool (many of which are purchasable for less than $100.00 - there are even some shareware ones out there - including one you can use found on YouTube itself) and then you create a voice recording (using an audio editor to improve it as required). The audio spans the time you allow people to view all the collective images and it plus your images becomes your sales pitch. You get to say what you want about the product and the audio with the images popping up as you go through your narrative becomes your video ad.

You then intersperse YouTube "Annotations" and "Cards' that contain your links and you can send people to your websites and sales or signup pages, to other YouTube playlists or videos you would like them to view, etc. Once uploaded to YouTube, you can go into editing mode and click on the "Promote" button to get the word out at 2-3 cents a paid click. So you don't have to spend a lot on an advertising video unless you want to which opens up YouTube as an advertising platform for everyone, including those running small at home businesses.

Now let's talk about the different ways you can advertise on YouTube.

- First, you create your own video and upload it to YouTube to your own channel and playlists and then promote it as I've already discussed above. One trick to consider is that if you do not monetize your ad video, you don't run the risk of someone else's add being placed on or around yours and thus having your potential customer being siphoned off to someone else's site.

- Second, you can use the YouTube system to advertise on and around your own ad video, just as if you were an external advertiser advertising on your video. This is kind of a double whammy approach to advertising, but some advertisers like to do this for the added advertising power you can build around the video and this strategy does work to gain more clicks from more viewers but it does cost you a little more to have the second campaign running as well.

- You can advertise on other creator's videos through one of two methods. First, you can connect with the other creator and strike a deal to have them weave your ad into their creations. This is not the usual approach for this but it does have the benefit of building collaborations with other creators and gets your ad in effect endorsed by the other content creator. They make some money directly from you via a side deal and you gain an endorsement and a higher quality level access to their entire subscriber base - which is in effect target marketing for you in niches you want to promote your product(s) in. The second method of course, is to use the YouTube marketing system to place ads on and around the videos of other creators who have monetized their content. Less targeting ability this way and no creator endorsement opportunities, but it is a cheap way to get the word out.

- You can also purchase space and run banner ads across the YouTube site. Their preferred size for these banner ads by the way, is 300 by 250 pixels. These ads will appear on many viewing pages and are not specifically tied to your channel or playlists.

- If you are a bigger advertiser or are willing to take on the additional costs, you are also able to create other more targeted ads with YouTube but you would then be working with a YouTube sales representative to negotiate these ads. One type of ad in this category that is gaining more and more traction these days is advertising directly against the YouTube mobile platform offering. YouTube is now working with advertisers to create offerings specifically targeting this space.

In any event, YouTube is out there waiting for you to promote your ads economically to its millions of viewers. You just have to pick the strategy you want to employ to get your ads out there.

OPTIMIZING YOUTUBE FOR YOUR BUSINESS

There are many different ways that you can reach your target audience online. You may choose to interact on several social media channels. Only you can decide which ones work the most effectively for you. You can also choose to use YouTube to post compelling videos. Videos will satisfy those target audience members who are visual.

Why YouTube?

You may not be aware that YouTube is an extraordinarily popular social media channel and billions of people go to the YouTube website regularly (around the world). Of course, it is understood that making a video comes with its own set of challenges. That is especially true if you have never made a video or have very limited experience in that area. If that is the case, you will need to establish your comfort zone when it comes to making videos for business. There are several step that you will most likely find helpful when it comes to creating videos for business and evoking the sort of reaction that you are looking for.

- Choose your keywords and key phrases carefully: Before you do anything else at all, you will need to choose your keywords. Make sure that you choose them very carefully. You can make use of the YouTube Keyword Tool, which will make choosing your keywords and key phrases relatively easy. That tool allows you to track the number of queries you have received (related to searches) in any given month. The way that it works is that you type in a keyword or key phrase and select "exact" to find out the number of people who are looking for your exact keyword or key phrase. That will give you a strong sense of whether you are hitting the mark the way that you should be.

- Know your competitors: As is the case with any social media channel, it is very important that you understand who your competition is and what they are doing or what they have that can trump you. Whichever number of results appears is basically the number of competitors that you have. It is an easy way to gauge. Of course, that means that you wand as small a number of videos as possible to show up! The keyword search tool is very effective and once you have performed the initial search, you can go back and hone your searches.

- Create the shell for your video: You are now at the stage where you can name your video file and create a thumbnail image. As always, you should consider content king. It truly is that. When it comes to how content is received (and viewed) by the search engines, they don't recognize images. They only recognize and rank text. That is extremely important to remember. With that in mind, you need to understand that a keyword in your video file name is extremely important for search engine optimization (SEO). It is very easy to make that happen with a video that you post on YouTube. As far as your thumbnail is concerned, you should strive to make it as enticing as possible. You will be happy with the results if you can manage to do that. Of course, it is critical that you don't only share an enticing thumbnail and then disappoint your target audience because your video has fallen short.

- Don't forget the meta tags, video description, and video title: When it comes to creating the most effective title possible, you should strive to have your title no more than 100 characters. The writing should be short and clear. It is also important that you remember to include a keyword in your title. When it comes to the specifications of your video description, it has been proven to be most effective if you place a keyword or key phrase in the first and last sentence. Those two places are where the keywords/key phrases will get the most attention. That may earn you higher search engine rankings. Now onto the meta tags. With YouTube, you can tag your video with the most effective keywords/key phrases.

- Use closed captioning: You might have seen closed captioning on television programs (or at least the option of it). It is a good thing to include with your video because it allows more of your target audience members to have the opportunity to view what you are sharing. It also is an effective way to get the search engines to pick up your content. It is an easy and effective way to increase your visibility online.

- Use calls-to-action: Of course, it goes without saying that you don't have total control over how many people actually view your video and whether those people choose to interact with you. However, you can provide them with the opportunity to interact with you. You can do that by providing a call-to-action that will make it as easy for them to interact with you as possible. In your call-to-action, you should either ask them for what you want or give them something that will enhance their interactions with you. You can use similar calls-to-action as you would in a written article. You can ask a thought-provoking question, leave an insightful comment, etc. People will probably be more than willing to share their opinions with you.

- Once your video is complete, embed it: It is very important for you to embed your video on your website for maximum exposure and buzz. You will need to optimize the page on your website where you have chosen to embed the video and that is an excellent way to build your credibility. Your video is showing instead of telling people about your business and demonstrating what you can do and what you are capable of doing for them.

Conclusion

If you follow the steps that have been outlined here, you will create and share a successful video that will get a lot of positive attention. YouTube is an excellent social media channel and you owe it to your business to take full advantage of it to bring your business to the next level. From the beginning, it is critical that you have a video content strategy outlined and you should make sure to stick with it on a permanent basis. Of course, it is also very important to remember that you are not in a world by yourself and without other people, you will not have a successful business. With that in mind, you must remember that if other people have been instrumental in your success, you should make sure to acknowledge their contribution in some way.

POWER OF FACEBOOK MARKETING FOR PRODUCT LAUNCHES AND AFFILIATES

Facebook started out as a social networking site mainly intended for personal use. Its aim was simply to provide a platform for people to share their thoughts, photos, videos, and to interact with people. However, the administrators have eventually expanded to more features. Facebook fan pages are intended for personalities and companies to share their information to their consumers and fans. So when you create Facebook fan pages, you allow the user to share information to a different degree, given their different features. Facebook marketing is a proof that a business can succeed through online activity. Celebrities, organizations, and retailers depend on Facebook for marketing.

Facebook marketing is a very effective way to build your presence. It's relatively easy, since all you need is a computer. You can create Facebook fan pages and a Social Ad. You are going to specify to Facebook the kind of audience that you want to reach and where the traffic should be directed. Using Facebook for marketing is helpful because Facebook helps you locate your audience through age, gender, location, and interests. Facebook's widespread popularity is ideal for increasing your chances of capturing the awareness of your desired audience. Contact-to-contact association will help spread your products and services via referrals. Facebook also allots a section where certain ads show up on the side portion of their user's window.

Another benefit of Facebook marketing is the significantly lowered costs of marketing and advertising by almost half. More people are now relying on the internet than the print, television, and radio (although these platforms still matter). However, you can make yourself more reachable to your audience if you use a Facebook marketing tool. This is a great way to boost your online presence and complement your official website. Overall, Facebook marketing is the good tool for expanding your lists because Facebook has over 500 million active users and spend at least 700 billion minutes browsing Facebook every month. Moreover, the typical Facebook user keeps in touch with at least 80 groups, events, and pages.

Building Your List with Facebook

The most basic element of Facebook marketing is the Facebook fan page. Once you've put up your own fan page, you can invite people to Like your fan page. Members of your fan page will get constant updates when they open their Facebook account.

When you open the Facebook website, create a fan page by going to Pages. Click Create a page. It's very important to keep your fan page busy and updated with the latest details about your product or service. Post blogs or articles regularly on your wall, preferably things that are related to your product or service. You are going to fill your page with your brand so you have to decide what stays in the page and what doesn't. Fill out the most important information about your product and include a relevant profile picture. Keep the About section brief but comprehensive. Facebook marketing should be accessible to the audience so you have to make your fan page readable so your logos and graphics should be kept to a minimum.

Building lists using the Facebook marketing method involves interaction with the people. If you want to widen your list base, you have to be the first one to reach out to your audience. You can start by liking related pages to your product or service. Interact with other people by initiating and participating in discussions. Answer questions, polls, and surveys. Ask questions too, if possible. Any kind of information in those pages should be valuable because you will rely on it for information on how to improve your own page and Facebook marketing.

Once you've gathered a considerable fan base, encourage the members to talk by initiating polls, surveys, and questions yourself. Keep the fan page active and updated. Be friendly with your replies too.

Express gratitude for positive comments and handle negative comments well. You cannot expect to please everyone so use those comments as a way to improve yourself.

Facebook Ads

A huge part of Facebook marketing is the Facebook Ads that you find on the right side of your profile page or your friends page. The Ads that you see pretty much speaks of what the person is all about. Facebook Ads are aimed at the person's age, education, location, and other interests based on the activity of the user. Advertisers usually promote their product based on a target group of people.

Payment of Facebook Social Ads varies, but the usual method is the pay-per-click method. You also have the option of activating a campaign, especially if there are certain times of the day or night when it is most profitable.

Facebook Ads are very easy to make. Go to facebook.com/advertising. Enter your website on the destination URL tab. Create a headline and an ad copy. Afterwards, post a relevant image for your ad. Once you've reviewed the visible details of your ad, it's time to work on the targeting filters. Setting your target filters is very important because it will determine the type of people who will advocate and patronize your product. You will target the geography of the people who will see the ads, as well as the sex, age, education, relationships, language, group and page membership, application usage, and other activities. Facebook will show you an estimated number of people you will be targeting. If you are not satisfied, you can always tweak the filters.

Once you're done, create a budget, bid, metrics and schedule of the page.

Conclusion

Facebook marketing is an exciting field of marketing and advertising products that can be pulled off by almost by anyone. However, the competition is going to be tough since it is accessible to everyone. But the thing is, you have to get the hang of using Facebook for marketing because people use this as a platform to connect with the world around them. The best way to start is to create a Facebook fan page. However, it doesn't stop there. People spend a lot of time online doing many things so you have to give them a good reason why you're worth their time. Constantly evolve and keep yourself updated. Remember, a well-maintained Facebook fan page attracts a large following.

USEFUL FACEBOOK MARKETING STRATEGIES TO UP YOUR INCOME

Like many other social networks, Facebook is an effective tool in any marketer's arsenal. But if you want to be successful with this tool, then you need to know how to use it.

Keep in mind that Facebook marketing is different from how the marketing on other social networking sites is done. This is because each tool has its specific purpose.

Just as you wouldn't use a wrench to hammer in a nail, you need to be aware of how to use Facebook correctly so that you don't waste your time or your money on marketing efforts that will ultimately end in a time and money failure.

Use Facebook to Drive Traffic to an Affiliate Promotion

There are three marketing strategies that you can use to make you more money on Facebook. The first method involves driving people to an affiliate promotion. If they click through your Facebook post or ad and make a purchase, then you'll get a commission.

Many marketers offer a commission rate of 50%, but you should never choose a product based solely on the commission rate. If you promote crappy products, users will catch on and you'll end up permanently damaging your brand for some quick cash.

That's not what you want to do if you're in the Internet marketing industry for the long haul. When it comes to promoting a product to make affiliate sales on Facebook, there are several things that you'll want to consider.

The first is whether this product will help your audience. If it doesn't meet a need or fulfill a want, then you might not find anyone who would want to buy it. And you could end up losing a lot of cash if you use boosted ads to promote the wrong product to the wrong audience.

Once you've established that a product really will help your followers, you need to evaluate the product yourself. As an affiliate, your name is on the line, too. If one of your followers buys this product and it doesn't deliver the results that were promised, your reputation will be tarnished in their eyes.

One unhappy customer will always tell others. It's far better to spend half an hour skimming the content of the product you plan to promote than it is to lose the trust and loyalty of your followers.

Now that you've confirmed that the quality of the product you'll be promoting really will help your customers, you need to exam the creator's sales page. There are some marketers who are so eager to launch their product, they don't pay enough attention to their sales page.

As a result, they have a great product that nobody will buy because of a poor landing page. If a sales page isn't going to convert readers into buyers, then there's no reason to pay to promote it to your own fans.

The only exception to this rule is if you've built a loyal audience that trusts your word and is willing to buy a product that has a vague or poorly worded sales page. But be careful about promoting products with bad sales pages too often.

You might even be able to contact the seller and ask for something specific to be set up just for your readers. You might even create a page yourself if they don't have the skills and ask them to use that for your orders only.

When it comes to Facebook posts, pictures are what capture your audience because we live in a more visual world than ever before. Yes, you need great sales text in your ad.

But if your picture doesn't capture the attention of your fans, they won't pause long enough to read your text. This is why picking an appropriate picture to include with your ad is so important.

Sometimes, you can use a photo directly from the sales page if it's a high quality image. Other times, the product creator may have "swipe" files available with images that you can attach to your post.

But not every marketer is great with graphics. Maybe they were in a rush to launch and something went wrong with their graphics delivery - or maybe they didn't take the time to hire someone who could create professional images.

When the images related to a product aren't great, you still have two options. You can create your own images by using a website like PicMonkey.com or Canva.com. Both of these websites will allow you to create nice graphics, even if you have no prior experience.

If you don't have the time or don't want to create your own images, you can also purchase a photo. Stock sites like depositphotos.com have millions of images that you can buy and use in your advertisement.

The content portion of your ad is important as well. Don't worry about the length of your content - here's why. What you really want to do is give the reader a feeling that they're reading a real review from a real person.

One way to do that is to personalize your review. For example, if you're promoting a product that will help your audience lose weight without giving up donuts and other junk food, then you might start your review by mentioning the day you had a meltdown because you'd failed your diet again.

By starting a review with a personal story, you help your readers lower their guard and make them more likely to click through and buy the product that you're referencing because they feel you can relate to them.

Keep in mind that a review that's too glowing and over the top time after time may put readers on the defensive. This is why it can be helpful to list both the pros and the cons of the product.

For example, you may mention that the diet program is great at giving you practical tips that you can use right away, but that you wish the course had focused on what to do if you're an emotional eater as well - or you wish it gave a set of recipes to incorporate into the plan.

Once you've finished up your review, you can create your Facebook post. But before you do, look at where you'll be directing your audience to go once they click on your ad. Don't direct them to a post on your blog where they can then click through to the product.

This adds an extra step to the sales process and makes them more likely to abandon their purchase before they complete it. Instead, you should have the link for your advertisement direct to the sales page of the product.

This means you'll have fewer buyers losing their way - and as a result, you should be earning plenty of affiliate commissions. Keep in mind that nobody on Facebook signs up to a page to be sold to 24/7.

Your affiliate posts and ads should be sprinkled in among many valuable posts that share free tips and insight with your Facebook fans.

Whenever you share good products and posts with your audience, the chance of them sharing it with their followers increases.

One of the great things about affiliate income through Facebook is that you have the potential to promote both tangible and digital products. If you're in the diet niche, for example, you can review both.

You might do a review of an info course from ClickBank one week - an ongoing review, or maybe even a challenge for your group. The next week, you might post a review of the new treadmill or barbells you just bought off Amazon.

Facebook is a great way to get going with your affiliate sales if you don't yet have a website of your own. You attract some like-minded people to your page, pepper them with good advice, and periodically promote what you deem acceptable to your followers.

Build a List Through Facebook

Facebook posts aren't just useful for earning affiliate commissions. They can also be used to grow your email list. As a marketer, one of the best things you can do is to focus on your subscriber volume.

These are people in your niche who are eager to hear from you and have given you permission to email them information. While growing your email list may not necessarily make you any money today, it can help you earn money later on.

This is because subscribers allow you to sell to them in the future many times over. So, while you may miss out on the opportunity for immediate cash, you can nurture a valuable relationship with subscribers and turn them into future buyers.

Before you purchase your Facebook advertisement or make an organic post, you should focus on creating a freebie. You want to offer your potential subscribers an opt in offer they can't ignore.

In order to come up with this freebie, you'll need to discover what buyers in your niche want most. You can start your research by looking at forums in your industry. For example, if you're in the pain management industry, then look for chronic pain forums.

Then begin looking for similar threads made by the forum users. You'll use these threads to note patterns and how users describe their aches and pains. This information will be helpful when you go to write your report.

From hundreds of forum threads, you might notice that the number one complaint on the forum is that back pain limits most users' activities. You could take this information and create a freebie around this need.

Your freebie might be about how to live with back pain without letting it take over your life and robbing you of daily activities like walking and running. But you'll still need to go beyond that.

You don't want a report that sounds generic, like it could have been written by just anybody. You want the report to capture your voice and more importantly, your story. Many marketers are in their niches, not just because they heard they could make money in these niches, but because of a personal reason.

Maybe you don't live with debilitating back pain, but you do know what it's like to live with chronic pain every day - or you had a short-term back injury that's since healed. Whatever made you decide to enter your niche, you need to tap into that well while writing your report.

You need to draw from your own experiences and you need to be real about it. Talk about the day when you were in so much pain you couldn't bend down to help your toddler tie his shoes.

Or that moment when you realized you had to give up your painting hobby because arthritis pain robbed you of the ability to hold a paint brush. These are the sort of things that will leave your reader nodding along and saying, "Wow, this person gets it! They understand how awful I'm feeling!"

When you've created that kind of feeling in your reader, they'll be connected to you. They'll look forward to your messages and they may even email you because they do feel like because you've been there, and you can help.

After you've created your report, it's time to get people to subscribe to your email list. Facebook posts are a great way to drive traffic to your sign up page, but you need to create your post or ad correctly.

Write the content of your ad focused on what your potential subscriber needs. Using the pain management example from above, you want your post to discuss how hard it is to live with back pain and how helpless this condition can leave your reader.

You want to show empathy here and that you understand exactly how your reader feels. Then pitch your report as the solution to the reader's problems and include a strong call to action that tells readers exactly what you want them to do.

For example, you might tell readers to, "Click here for your free life-changing report today!" After you have the content for your Facebook post, you'll want to choose where readers go after clicking on your link.

You want to send them to a squeeze page. This page should have a compelling headline, bullet points designed to remind your reader of the value of this freebie, and possibly a short video.

Your video doesn't have to be complicated or fancy. In fact, readers may relate to you more if you're in your home office, chatting with them like you would if you were having coffee together.

This will reassure potential subscribers that you're authentic and trustworthy. The final element that you need for your opt-in page is your email form. You only need to include two fields on this form - one for your subscriber's name and one for their email address.

Adding more fields makes it more likely that your visitor won't subscribe. If needed, you can always email your subscriber later and ask them for more information. But for now, you should stick with just the two fields.

Once you've finished with your opt-in page, you can submit your post to Facebook and watch your mailing list grow even bigger.

Now this is when you want to post about your opt in offer and possibly boost the post for more exposure to those who haven't yet become Fans of your page yet. But there's another way to grow your list on Facebook.

You'll have people who join your page, and from there, they can opt in directly on your Facebook Fan page! If you're using Aweber, for example, log into Facebook and click this link to add the Aweber app to Facebook.

Choose your page from the drop down and click Add Page Tab. This will take you back to your page. On the left side of your page, you'll see the Email Sign Up button, which you want to click on.

Click Configure - and enter your Aweber login details. Allow access and press configure again. Choose the list and form you want to use and Save changes!

Use Facebook to Drive Traffic to Your Product Offers

Another way you can use Facebook is to drive traffic to one of your own product offers and increase your income by creating a scarcity mindset. This is important because consumers are overwhelmed with information.

Unless you give them an incentive to click right now, users are going to navigate right past your post. One way to create a scarcity mindset is to limit your offer by the number of copies available.

In your post or advertisement, you might say that you only have fifty licenses of your product to sell. Don't lie, obviously, but if it's a limited number of available copies, that can be enough to make them take action now instead of planning on coming back later.

Mention that you know these licenses will go fast, if they will. Just like that, you've made your reader think that if they don't take action right now, they'll be missing out on something.

You can also create a scarcity mindset by making your offer time sensitive. This works well if you've just released your product. You might tell readers that the introductory price to your product will only last for a short period of time - like forty-eight hours.

Keep in mind as you write your post that it's a mini sales page. But you need to avoid hyping up your offer. This might be seen as spammy and social networks are all about sharing, not selling.

This means that too much hype could backfire on you and result in poor sales numbers. You'll also want to briefly mention your reader's needs and why this is the perfect solution for them.

A selling point might be that your product is easy. If your product isn't easy, maybe the selling point is that it's fast. For example, you might tell readers that your diet plan promotes healing of the gastric system in just two weeks.

Whatever your selling point is, mention it in your Facebook post. Finally, you want to include a special incentive for readers who click through from Facebook. There are many incentives that you could offer, but one popular item is a discount coupon.

Make sure that this discount coupon is time-sensitive. You don't want your reader taking a lot of time to think before purchasing your offer and seeing it closed. Another incentive that you might prefer to include is a special page, set up with a bonus that's just for buyers from Facebook.

Don't throw junk at your customers just so you can say that you have a bonus. You want your bonus to be an item that's actually valuable and really will help your customers.

But you don't have to make your bonus a product, it could also be a service. For example, you might offer a free hour of coaching for Facebook buyers or give them a free review of their website.

Not only does this give your buyer an exclusive bonus, but it also gives them a chance to work with you one on one. If you're a service provider, you could then pitch your services to these buyers later, after they've accepted your bonus offer. This can result in even more income from that one Facebook sale.

You should learn how to use these three strategies with both organic posts and boosted ads on Facebook. You'll want to learn the guidelines about what's allowed and what's not, but sometimes writing a really good organic post and boosting it can result in more sales than a hyped up typical "advertisement" because it allows those reading your post to connect with you on a more trustworthy level.

Facebook marketing is a great way to reach a wide base of potential customers. Just remember that like all marketing endeavors, your goal should be to provide value. If you do that, then you'll continue to grow your business, your subscriber list, and ultimately, your income.

FACEBOOK MARKETING TIPS FOR BUSINESS

Many business executives recognize the value of marketing on Facebook and have taken the first step by developing a Facebook Fan Page for their business. But after the page is created, many CEO's drop the ball and do not take full advantage of all that Facebook has to offer for their business. So, we have compiled a list of marketing tips for business owners.

Posting on Other Business Pages

Facebook Fan Pages have evolved into a place where Pages can post and update on other Pages. In "Page" mode, you can like and comment on other pages. In Page mode you can write on the profiles of your friends. Wall posts are no longer in chronological order, and we do not really have a lot of control on the posts on our Pages. The good news as a Facebook admin is that you can "view" your page in chronological order. To do this under "wall" click "admin view". This helps you to organize your own page by viewing it in the order that is easiest to understand and manage.

As you are in "page view mode", if the name of your fan page is not your real name, as is the case with most fan pages (they are the name of the business), it is important to add an identity to your post. If you are commenting on other fan pages, go ahead and sign off at the end of your comment with a dash and your first name. This helps to add a personal touch to your posts and improves your engagement factor.

Think about how you are coming across. Are you at your competitors' pages because of self-serving agenda or are you there to contribute? We recommend that you do most of your networking in a business industry that is not the same as your business (a non-competitive industry). You can post on the pages of businesses that are related to yours, but not your competitors. You might get more results that way.

Prevent Spam on your Own Page

Many business owners have noticed that, at times, their competitors will spam their page. Facebook now has spam filters that you can use to curve this. In order to access and utilize Facebook spam filters, you can find this tool under "edit page" and it allows you to load keywords that are put into the spam filter so you, as the admin, can automatically filter posts. This is located in "admin view". Comments show up in a light color which some people have said is more difficult to see, however, this tool is still very useful.

Notifications can be by email or you can turn that off by clicking "edit page". This is helpful because as you get new fans or comments you can get notifications.

Marketing Tips

1. Photo Strip at the top of your Page.

The photos at the top of your page are the five photos that are the most recently uploaded. You can delete them by clicking the X in the right hand corner of each page.

The "Photo Strip" at the top acts like a photo viewer and the photos pop up so the viewer does not lose their place when looking at photos. Have some custom graphics made for the top 5 photos on your page. They can be 970 x 680 pixels. We recommend that you leave white space around the edges of the photos. FB will shrink them to a 97 x 68 thumbnail. Use images with a call-to-action such as "click here", "find out more", "get details", or "free download". When visitors click on that image, the image will pop up. In the description of that image, put details and a call-to-action with a link or your phone number so visitors can easily contact you.

2. Links along the left-hand section of your Page.

Reset the order of your links on the left-hand side of your Facebook Page. If you have more than 7, you will see a "more" link and from there you can drag and drop those links. Put the "landing tab" at the bottom which is usually a "welcome" where visitors land. This way when they visit your welcome page, all your links will automatically be expanded and they can see your entire list of all your links along the left-hand section of your page.

3. Take advantage of Facebook iFrames by adding interesting content.

Facebook uses iFrames and although it is a little more complex, it gives you the ability to add images, videos and opt-in boxes and a call to action. You can have a whole page designed on your own site and then post that in your iFrame within your Facebook page and make that your custom landing tab. In addition, you can take Facebook ads out and drag them specifically to landing pages and links on your Facebook page. This gives you the ability to test different promotions and offers. You can experiment and split test with your different offers on different iFrames links on your page.

4. Updates feature offers the opportunity of free advertising in valuable Facebook real-estate.

Click "edit page" "marketing". You can send all of your fans updates. All these communications go into "other". On the top right-hand corner of Facebook, you will see an area called "Unread Updates". This is valuable real-estate so that if you use "updates" more frequently, you can get your fans more interested in your fan page. If you have a very active post on your wall, you can take that exact link and add that into the "updates" so that your fans will see that on the top right-hand corner of their page. By using "updates" you will have free ads for yourself and it appears on the top right-hand corner of your fans' pages.

5. Increase visibility and engagement with Facebook News Feeds.

Studies show that Up to 90% of your fans do not return to your page after they click the "like" page. Not to worry, however, because by maximizing your visibility in Facebook News Feed, you can still be visible to your fans and engage them in order to "remind" them about your business and increase visitors to your main web site, which after all, is the next step in increasing your bottom line.

Your fans can see your content in their news feed. But the question is "how do your get your content visible in your fan's news page?".

Facebook uses a very complex algorithm (called "edge rank"), so we don't know exactly why some posts show up in news feeds and some do not, but we do know what can increase your visibility in your fans' news feed.

Tips to increase your visibility in your fans' news page include:

- Post before noon in your time zone.
- Post 1 to 2 times a day. Do not over post. Some companies import tweets and "over post". This can hurt your "edge rank", (the algorithm that Facebook uses), which can ultimately lead to your posts showing up less and less in your fans' news feed.
- Use questions.
- Keep posts short and simple.
- Be personal.
- Use other people's content. Include photos, videos, and links. Create your own strategies to increase your visibility in news feeds.

By utilizing these tips, you can increase visibility on Facebook and engage more fans.

OVERCOMING FACEBOOK MARKETING MYTHS

Many people try to avoid using Facebook to market their business. They don't really know enough about Facebook and how effective it can be for marketing purposes. Some of the more popular myths will be dispelled here.

If you are looking for a great way to really increase your visibility and reputation online, Facebook is an excellent way to do it. It has a phenomenal number of users and they are growing in number all of the time. When you think about that in terms of growing your business, it makes no sense whatsoever for you not to get involved (as a business person) with Facebook.

The following are some of the myths that people have bought into about Facebook.

- Only kids use Facebook: Many people believe that Facebook has no benefits for business because the largest part of its demographic is young. That has actually started to change. The older demographic (35) of Facebook has grown dramatically

118

and is still increasing to this day.

- You are too old for Facebook: At the other end of the spectrum from the myth above, in addition to the demographic now being older, age has very little to do with your successful use of Facebook. All that really matters is that you have something to say that is valuable and interesting to other people with whom you connect online. If anything, older age can be an advantage because with age comes wisdom and insight.

- Using Facebook is too time-consuming: Regarding the amount of time that is necessary to make Facebook work for your business, it all depends on how you manage your time. If you put yourself on a structured schedule and you really are committed to sticking to that schedule, the amount of time that you devote to Facebook does not have to be overwhelming and all consuming. The benefits that you will receive from spending the time and effort far outweigh any disadvantages that you can think of. In order to get the most out of your Facebook time, it is best to have a strategy in mind before you even start. Ask yourself what your strategy is and which goals you hope to achieve by interacting with people on Facebook. It is very important to have a clear understanding of why you are actually using Facebook to interact.

- All you need is Facebook to get clients: We all wish that this were true. However, it usually takes more effort than that to build up your business and acquire new clients. Unfortunately, many people believe this myth and are so disappointed when it doesn't happen that way that they totally give up on Facebook after that. Facebook should be a part of your overall marketing strategy. It cannot be the entire strategy. Facebook is a great way to demonstrate your credibility and expertise. As you start to build relationships through Facebook, people will come to trust you and to turn to you for answers to their questions and solutions to their problems because they will consider you to be the expert.

- If you have a personal profile on Facebook, you don't need anything else: This is a myth that many people accept as the truth. You should have a personal Facebook page that includes friends and family and a Facebook Fan Page that you use solely for business purposes. It is very important to separate the two. You certainly don't want your business associates to know about the details of your life that is personal in nature. Facebook fan pages are public whereas Facebook pages are private. Because fan pages are public, the search engines can detect them and can rank them accordingly. You can also use your fan page to spread the word (virally) about your business offerings and your brand.

Tips to help you to get a lot out of Facebook without putting a lot into it

- Turn off most of your alerts: Based on your schedule, your goal is to spend a specific (and relatively short) amount of time on Facebook. If you leave all of your alerts on and you receive frequent notifications that tell you when someone has reached out to you, you will become very distracted and you will end up spending more time on Facebook (most likely for non-business purposes) than you should or than you intended.

- Ignore meaningless applications: Facebook has a great deal of applications that are fun but that serve no purpose for you when it comes to business. It is different if you want to get involved with them in your "play" time.

- Update your status on a regular basis: You should choose regular intervals to update your status and if something significant changes in your status in between those intervals, you should update it as it happens also.

- Peruse your newsfeeds: You should pay regular attention to your news feeds, which consist of the status updates of your Facebook connections, and if something is of interest to you, either share it with others or make a comment on it.

- Respond quickly: If someone has placed a comment on your wall, respond in kind with a comment of your own. You should respond as quickly as you can.
- Announce your events: If you are involved with an event, share the information with other people. You should try to get as many people as possible involved.
- Share your blog: Use the NetworkedBlogs or Notes application to import your blog postings, which will subsequently in your Facebook fans news feeds.

What do you do next?

- Continually update your page with fresh content: An effective way to accomplish this is by posting blog articles on a very regular basis.
- Pose questions that require answers from other people: It is very important to engage your readers as much as possible. The more engaged you make them; the more discussions will be generated.

- Be good to your fans: Allow your fans to take advantage of your business offerings, including special promotions, events and free giveaways.

- Communicate: Let your fans know what you are up to in your business and allow them to interact with you regularly.

Conclusion

After reading this article, you have hopefully been convinced that what you might have been feeling and what you believed about Facebook for business are not true. You can use Facebook for your business and all that it has to offer. So, jump right in and start connecting.

FACEBOOK MARKETING IDEAS AND TOOLS

In today's fast paced life every aspect of business and money making seems to be up-graded every now and then. Today one of the most extensively used medium of communication as well as business is the internet. Therefore it does not come as a surprise that this medium has over the years developed and designed newer and more effective ways of doing business by either creating new or generating from the existing segments, ideas and tools that would benefit the business entity using this vast system. One of the main intentions of the internet is to make work both easy and rewarding. More often than not people operating on the net have contributed towards this goal and have provided the general public, small production groups as well as big companies with ways and means to market their services and products which are both hassle free and cost effective. One such avenue on the internet is the social networking sites, and amongst those 'Facebook' is the most prominent. Not only does it have one of the highest member populations world-wide but it also boasts of probably the highest number of non-individual profiles or group/company profiles. So it's not surprising that it has been seeing a lot of marketing based activity and that too with success. But the most effective ones are those which are done on a selected, tried and tested patterns, some of which will be shared with you in this segment.

To start one needs to create a profile page on Facebook. It is to be remembered that this profile would be the face with which people across the globe would be recognizing you. Hence, care should be taken while creating a profile and it should have some source of attraction to lure visitors and make them read it.

Being a networking site, Facebook obviously works with creating a network including as many numbers of peoples and profiles as possible. Therefore it is necessary for your profile to enlarge its reach. There are various ways to do this like creating a connecting chain and also groupings and communities.

Groups and communities form a major center of marketing activities and can be utilized for great results. You can create a group of your own or participate in an existing community to present about your products and services and then have reviews and debates on the same. It leads to rich publicity.

Status updates on your profile can also be of great use in this regard. As most of the people follow each other via status updates, it could be used to send across more informative messages about your brand or services. Even links and video files could be uploaded to deliver the requirements via status updates.

Using interesting titles and descriptions on your profile page might just turn out to be the difference between people ignoring or clicking your post. So it is apparently advisable to adorn your profile with attractive titles and even more captivating descriptions so as to get the attention of even a casual surfer.

Heeding to the demands of the marketing users, Facebook came up with the idea of pages a couple years ago. These pages are a great medium for business especially the small and medium scale ones to make their presence felt on the social network. Moreover various other soft wares like flash and other applications of Facebook apart from HTML can be added on to the page. So it can be customized and utilized to the optimum.

Paying attention to user response and examining it every now and then would go a long way in establishing your brand of products or services. Small details like whether or not there is an increase in the traffic of visitors or what are the comments and reviews shared by them on your profiles would help you to enhance your standards and in turn leave an indelible effect on your brand.

One thing has to be taken good care of if you want to get the optimum best out of Facebook is that you don't need to sell in the face to be a good marketing strategist. As a matter of fact with the Facebook public the principle of "90/10" fits to the hilt in terms of rejection to what is presented. How often have you yourself rejected any approach of sales? This indicates to the fact that Facebook is a social network and hence what would click here is that if one could present a solution to other's problems and the marketing would be done when they communicate to others.

One more method of the very basics is that one should give extra importance to the filling of the account settings and details. Mostly it's a tendency amongst people to scuttle through the various forms and jump up to get connected with other similar interest users or their friends. But it should be noted that the details of your profile are going to go a long way in establishing a connection between yourself and the visitor; therefore it should not only be complete but also explanatory. So, ample importance must be given to this activity.

Very often people out of habit or sheer fear of the competition do not reveal their ideas on such sites for social benefit. On the contrary this particular measure can serve you in good stead. Even if you share your ideas on a platform or amongst a community that also includes people with your kind of business interests, it's going to come very handy as you might come across as a specialist on the subject or someone who is an authority.

Putting up a link of your Facebook account on other sites that you may have or even blogs will do wonders to promote your profile and in turn your business. Most of the readers would definitely have a Facebook profile and it would be interesting for them to visit the profile of the person who owns the site or blog they are visiting albeit out of curiosity. This would undoubtedly increase traffic and in turn a word of mouth which would have an effect on your business.

Uploading videos is also a very effective tool in this context. A video that should not be an out an out marketing promo but a subtle way to deliver a remedy for certain problem would definitely hit the jack pot with the Facebook savvy public. It would sound friendlier and hence would attract rather than repel people at the first glance.

Another major tool that can be easily overlooked is the gathering of like minded individuals who can help expand your business. This is not to be confused with business groups or communities. In groups or communities you might find other types of members as well. Members who do not exactly help promote things actively but just were finding something benefiting them so they held on; therefore it becomes necessary to gather around people who have the same zeal for promoting the particular cause. They can provide the edge in the market of Facebook itself and enlarge your reach to an extent previously not manageable.

Amongst the other important but easily overlooked methods is the very essence of networking. Consider this that Facebook is a social site therefore what is there in your service or product that could be presented in the form of something beneficial for that virtual society. This is where generally such community marketing clicks. If it is presented in the correct fashion then it could get on and spread like wild fire.

Sticking to your ethics is what is going to get you the fair deal. Beware of venturing into anything that could lead your messages to be dumped in the spam section. Consider yourself what is it that you would rather dump there. It would be easier for you to grasp it then.

Apart from all this one also needs to be constantly checking as to what new has come up in the virtual market. For this it is mandatory that you keep track of the network and your own created network helps you here. In this regard the business ethics is the same as anywhere else. You have to be a step ahead of the market, in this case the virtual community.

Facebook boasts of various segments of the market on its pages or profiles. Almost all fields of business are there on it, be it financial or legal or consumer goods or travel or real estate or insurance you name it and they are there on Facebook. Therefore it shouldn't be a surprise that there are dedicated websites which are guiding people towards various ways and methods to utilize this site for the best of results. A glance at these sites would do no harm as a matter of fact it would boost your chances, however it also depends on your acumen as a business professional.

Apart from the profile ways there are also the old direct marketing ways like getting your banner posted on Facebook or one liner. The prospect of reaching to over two hundred million people in such a fashion could look easily allure anybody to do it, however here again the concept should not be over done ever. It could back fire on the brand if the people start getting irritated.

There are also firms that deal in compiling of emails of the members of Facebook and they also can be approached for a sort of a mutually beneficial tie up. Having the email ids of so many people from different parts of the world could prove to be a vital tool in your quest for expansion but here again the key is correct utilization. The approach is what predetermines the deal, if it clicks with the recipient then your can reap the rewards far more than you could imagine.

One can also set up a fan page on Facebook. This fan page is basically a profile open for public that empowers the brand with its growing fan base. It empowers it by getting it connected to the Facebook users and share it so as to enlarge the virtual market presence. But any such fan page should be made with a clear vision and a studied content, what it that you want to present and to what extent is do you wish to share with your prospective customers and clients. Constant updating of the page is also must as it is the face of your brand.

Various incentives can also be used to propel business and generate traffic to the fan page or company profile page. For e.g. you can run a strategy that offers 'n' number of rewards for people who have successfully expanded the reach of the page amongst their friends and connections on the network by making them a member of the profile or fan page. These help in enlarging your fan base and as a result you could easily conduct any survey with better results that would serve your purpose in the true sense. Also you could use the survey or its tools as incentives or make it incentive based to generate more members. You need to keep all sorts of people in mind, it just might be that the fans of your page might need a bit more than what they are getting to promote your page or others might be offering something and they would get lured to that so why should you risk such a thing for so less. Therefore its advisable to offer any kind of incentives, it need not necessarily be monetary but it has to be something appealing enough.

Taking care of the current enrolled customers is of as much importance as looking for means and ways to create new ones if not more. Actually if only one would keep himself busy with the former that would suffice his requirements as these on roll customers would slowly but steadily and inevitably enlarge the reach if they are satisfied. As matter of fact they would do it sooner rather than later for there is nothing more infectious than a happy customer.

Finally, one should understand that Facebook is a tool and a society at the same time. The key is to strike the right balance between the two and reap the rewards for it big time.

GENERATING LEADS THROUGH LINKEDIN

What I find interesting is just how under estimated LinkedIn is. The more popular Facebook, Twitter, YouTube get all the hype and attention while this gold mine quietly sits and grows and grows. My guess is that because it is a professional networking site it doesn't have the universal sex appeal of the others, but a savvy sales and marketing executive knows - or should know the power of LinkedIn.

Generating more business is everyone's job at a company no matter what your position. Everyone should not only be a brand ambassador but should also be a lead magnet. LinkedIn is primo for the B2B market and even for B2C companies. When one conjures thoughts of vendors, strategic alliances, investors, allies, partners, employees, consultants and prospects, START with LinkedIn.

Market research reveals that it is the first place HR checks when either looking for or vetting a candidate. Statistics reveal that the education and earning levels of members is one of the highest of all the social media properties, with the exception maybe of practice specific sites for lawyers, accountants and the like. Becoming successful is not a result of hard work and smarts alone, it often boils down to 'not what you know, it is who you know' and LinkedIn will help you get those valuable connections.

So what can LinkedIn do for you and how can you start generating leads?

Before I venture into some of the lead generating activity suggestions, please spend some time on your profile and settings. Make sure that your profile is complete, that you are incorporating keywords in your titles and descriptions, and above all, make sure that you describe yourself in a way that clearly delivers the value in knowing you!

1. Grow your network: LinkedIn has tools that connect directly with Outlook and has the ability to search other email accounts to see who you know already on LinkedIn. If you don't connect your email program, at least perform a monthly check for new contacts in your database for who is on LinkedIn.

Tip: Every time you go to an event carry a small envelope with the date and name of the event. Place all the cards you collect into that envelope and when you get back to your office start reaching out to those people to connect and use a personalized message such as 'it was great meeting you yesterday at the EVENT, I would love to stay in touch and see how we might be of service to one another."

2. Updates: there is a feature much like Twitter and Facebook that allows you to post an update that will show up on your profile and in network updates to your connections. Use it wisely.

3. Introductions: Give them, ask for them. The idea of 6 degrees of separation is made apparent on LinkedIn. If there is a contact at a particular company you seek, by searching on LinkedIn you will discover who you already know that knows who you want to know. Introductions make a cold call a warm call and a faster track to closing a sale.

4. Get Visible: LinkedIn provides updates to members you are connected with. Some people adjust their updates to daily, some weekly but the point is that delivered to your connection's inbox are updates and you should find ways to have your name show up in those updates. Read on for some suggestions on how to accomplish this.

5. Referrals: say thanks to someone - a vendor, partner, even a customer - for a job well done or just acknowledging some special talent or skill that had a positive impact. Chances are they will reciprocate. And don't be shy about asking customers to write a recommendation but be careful to ask only those who have actually worked with you and can speak to your professional brilliance.

6. Groups: join groups that are relevant to your business and interests and that you can contribute to meaningfully. Groups where your prospects participate are a good place to start. Much like real life, hanging out with the right people is a solid step toward successful connections.

7. Books: LinkedIn provides the opportunity to mention what you are reading or have read with a short blurb regarding the book. I could write volumes on why this is a pivotal tool but for now just let me say that sharing this information is a really good idea.

8. Events: the events feature on LinkedIn lets you browse what is happening and in some cases, people will actually make notation that they are attending. You might just find that the person you are trying to meet will be at an event in your area.

9. Slideshare: has expanded to not just power point decks but now includes video and other documents. This is a great way to show off some of that industry specific knowledge that no one knows you have.

10. Blogs: LinkedIn can automatically pull in your blog posts. If you would like to grow your reader base, or just keep your contacts in the know with the great material you are providing through your blog, don't forget to activate this feature.

11. Twitter: ugh. Yes, LinkedIn will allow you to stream your tweets into your profile. I say ugh because I caution you as this can become annoying. I am not a fan of this feature as I find it clutters the page as most tweets are inane at best and often times out of context and offer no real value. Each person is different and it might work for you but I would exercise caution here.

12. Saved Search: if you want to keep tabs on a company you are interested in, conduct a search on that company and save it so that any changes with the people in that company will be in your updates. Are they letting more people go then hiring? Did someone get a promotion? Did they hire someone you know?

The take away: LinkedIn is a professional networking platform where the information is rich and powerful and the opportunity to break barriers of entry exists. A lot of searches are done on LinkedIn and this is another opportunity to get found by the people you want to find you. Link your way to success!

LINKEDIN MARKETING TIPS FOR THE NEWBIE

LINKEDIN TIP #1: COMPLETE YOUR LINKEDIN PROFILE

It doesn't matter if you are just starting out on LinkedIn, or you have been around the block for years, make sure you go through each step and complete your profile at least to the standards of LinkedIn by:

- Adding your picture (make it a clean and professional please.
- Add a compelling summary
- Give and receive a few recommendations
- Update your current and past work experiences (this will be a HUGE factor in a future tip)
- Add your Hobbies
- Add your Interests
- And so on...

Completing your profile makes you seem more consistent in your actions.

138

*Note: These principles will make or break your entire LinkedIn experience.

LINKEDIN TIP #2: WRITE ABOUT YOURSELF AND WHAT YOU DO:

One of the first things people look at when they see your profile is your headline, so it's important that you make sure you tell the viewer two things:

1. Who You Serve

2. How You Serve Them

This quicker you can get to giving people exactly what they need in the least amount of time, the more results you will receive.

Just be brief and to the point. The more specific you can be, the more of a targeted audience that will reach out to connect with you and ask you to help them (meaning pay you!). It's pretty amazing how YOUR profile can be the first result for words like "advertising" "sales coach" "social media" "product developer" and so on.

LINKEDIN TIP #3: SUMMARIZE YOUR LINKEDIN PROFILE

Your LinkedIn summary is the part that tells YOUR story (i.e. your skill set, what you have to offer, how people can work with you, etc.)

If you really want to see results using LinkedIn, make sure you put some energy into playing to your highest potential.

This is what I want you to do when it comes to completing your summary:

- Start with your intro paragraph stating who you are, your passions and your goals. This doesn't have to be long, but get people interested in you as an individual (remember, we do business with those we feel weKnow, Like, and Trust).
- Create a new paragraph and tell people exactly who you help.
- Create a new paragraph and tell people exactly how you help them.
- Create a new paragraph and tell people how to contact you.

Remember to keep it simple, personal (yes personal, this is not a resume... it is a SOCIAL networking site so make it social!).

If you do this you will be achieving your goals in no time my friend!

LINKED TIP #4: CUSTOMIZE YOUR PROFILE

It bugs me when people do not customize their website links on LinkedIn. Why? Because if just doesn't look right and you are not giving yourself the best chance to achieve your goals.

When you first create a profile it will read something like this:

- My Website
- My Website
- My Company
- Make sure you change it to read something more like this:
- Learn about my projects
- Follow My Tweets
- Get Free Articles

Having more of a "Call to Action" will drive more people to your websites, and ultimately drive traffic and bring you quality leads for your business.

To customize your websites just click on "edit" next to "your website", then on the drop down tab click on "other" and add what you want it to read.

LINKEDIN TIP #5: GET CONNECTED!

Sometimes the biggest opportunities I receive are from people I don't even know, but who have heard about me from someone else. Has this ever happened to you?

It happens to me all of the time on LinkedIn. Random people contact me and ask me what my bank account detail is so they can send me money for my services. Would you like to receive random emails like that? If you said "YES" then read on.

Here is what I want you to do:

1. Import all of your contacts into LinkedIn:

Import from Gmail, Outlook, Hotmail, and gather up all of your excel spread sheets and add them to your personal network on LinkedIn.

2. Send a mass personalized message:

This message lets them know you are updating your LinkedIn profile and that you would love to connect with them. By increasing your 1st degree connections you are actually expanding your 2nd and 3rd degree network... i.e. bringing you more opportunities for people who don't know you, to pay you MONEY! Therefore, add your current contacts to your LinkedIn profile, and start enjoying when people contact you out of thin air and help you build your business.

142

LINKEDIN #6: GET RECOMMENDATION FROM YOUR CONNECTIONS

I already know you understand this, but when someone you trust recommends someone to you, you are more than likely to believe that person has a lot of value because you respect the person vouching for them isn't it? This is true with getting recommendations on LinkedIn. The more recommendations you have, the more valuable and sought after you become because of all the trusted professionals who have vouched for you. How do you get lots of recommendations? You do this by giving a lot of quality recommendations to those that you can vouch for upfront, without asking for anything in return. By doing so, a majority of those people you wrote the recommendation for will feel it necessary to give you one in return. Just make sure that you don't recommend any stranger, and provide them for individuals you know, like, and trust. You will see that the more recommendations you give, the more you will receive and this will only help bring in more business and achieve your professional goals.

LINKEDIN TIP #7: THE POWER OF GROUPS

Do you know what it feels like to be on a team? You know... where you receive support from teammates, and follow the vision of the leader to achieve a common goal? It can be a powerful feeling being on a team, and there can be a huge benefit to you because of it. The LinkedIn groups section is sort of like being on a team. Just like facebook groups, there is a vision for each group, various members, job postings, news listings, a section to discuss ideas, and a leader who runs it all. The best part about being a member of groups is that you can contact each member for free, without having to know their email address. However, without being in the group with them, you would have to upgrade to a paid profile to contact them. And paying more to network with people isn't fun, so I wouldn't recommend it. So you actually save yourself money by simply joining groups.

ALTERNATE MLM STRATEGIES - LINKEDIN MARKETING

Today, LinkedIn is perhaps the most important professional networking platform. Launched in 2003, it had over 150 million users and from over 200 countries and territories, in hundreds of languages, as of February 2012. The best part about this site is that you find targeted professionals and groups directly. While using social media for marketing is not new, using LinkedIn Marketing for business has its own charm for its different set of rules.

As a self imposed code of conduct, I found individuals and group members to post content or comments in a very professional and cultured style. Exceptions apart, that happens anywhere. This aspect sets LinkedIn apart from the rest of social networking platforms. It place Linked as probably the best social media marketing tool for business.

For a serious marketer LinkedIn represents a unique and lucrative opportunity to market himself as a "brand". All MLM professionals recognize and understand the relevance of "Me Brand". The quality of your content and the value it brings to the group members, establishes you as an authority, a guru or a knowledgeable person on your topic.

Use LinkedIn for Business

The art of business promotion and making money from LinkedIn is not much different than for using social media for marketing sites like Facebook or Twitter. The advantage is that here you are interacting with your target group directly. To that extent the process of filtration of your contact group becomes easier and quicker. Further, the knowledge gap between you and your target group is much narrow. Of course, the quality and quantum of knowledge differs. It is this differential knowledge gap or lag that represents an opportunity for you to slip in your offer as a recommendation to the knowledge or help seeker. The rider being "provided he seeks your help".

I have often wondered why one does not see some of the otherwise active names from the MLM world on LinkedIn. Could it be that it is difficult to sell a "Rich by Click" product to a professional? A professional see through such scams. It is also difficult to offer products at $7.99 or 9.99 in hope of a backend up sale. A professional will not fall for these sleazy tricks.

Having said this, let's see the steps in the LinkedIn marketing process.

The principles remain the same. Generate Leads, Leads and more Leads.

There are two sources of attracting leads into your system, "Your Profile" and "Your Knowledge". Let's visit these factors.

Your Profile

Your profile is the strongest pull for leads. Attract leads through a professionally crafted profile. Unlike other social networking sites, at LinkedIn, your profile picture plays a very important role. Being a professional site it is formal. I would therefore recommend having a picture in a business jacket at least. The profile must be crisp and to the point, establishing you as an authority. Your profile picture, description, experience, education and achievements establishes you as a professional.

Now you must establish two more personality traits, "Integrity" and "credibility". For that you must have a number of recommendations from people with who you have worked before or companies you have dealt with. These recommendations act as your testimonials. All serious profile visitors go through the recommendations to gauge your capabilities and professional standing. I would strongly suggest that before setting up your profile, you go through the LinkedIn guide.

Knowledge - Your Content and Interaction within the Group

You must regularly post value added content. The quality of your interaction within the group will also act as an attraction. These actions will establish your professional credibility and invoke the curiosity to know more about you. You see what is happening...your content and social behavior is channeling people to your profile again - to your leads funnel.

My observation about LinkedIn culture is that people are expected to share knowledge through content, interactions, display of specific skills and so on. I have rarely seen people offering a product or an opportunity blatantly. This all happens behind the scene once you have the leads in your system.

Chase your Profile Viewers

As a daily routine, you should check who all visited your profile in the past 24 hours. These are the people who have walked that extra mile to your profile, the proof of their interest in you.

Let me ask you a simple question. When do you view someone's profile? Only when there is a curiosity about the person or when you want to connect with a person. In both cases, you have someone who has walked the way to your door. It is now your turn to take over and build a relationship.

Open the Door

Yes, if the person who viewed you profile is from your known group, the task becomes simple. After a cooling period of 24 hours or so, pick up the phone and talk to him. Just say "Hi, just connecting, it has been a while since we talked". The magic starts. You are getting a raw lead into your money funnel. From here on repeat the same tactics that you use in any other MLM script.

For those who viewed your profile and are not from your known group, the best way of breaking the ice is a direct message via LinkedIn. Inform the viewer that you were excited to find that he viewed your profile recently. Tell him on what you do and ask him if you could be on any help to them. You would see the magic unfolding over a period.

Leads to Recruit

The process of converting a lead into a recruit is the same, be it Facebook, Twitter or LinkedIn. You have to wait for the right opportunity to put forth your product to the lead when he or she requests you to.

This will give you the chance to convert the lead not only into a prospect but also as a recruit who gives you both residual and leveraged income.

LINKEDIN MARKETING - THE SECRET BEHIND SOCIAL NETWORKING SUCCESS

LinkedIn is a professional, business and career oriented social networking site. It allows you to meet professional experts in a variety of industries across the globe.

There's currently over 35 millions professionals on LinkedIn and these numbers are growing as we speak.

The LinkedIn community enables you to connect with like minded people which in returns allow you to grow your business contacts and network.

As a registered member, you get to create your own personal profile with information about you, your company, your products and services. You can also mention your professional accomplishments.

Once you've done this, you can begin to maintain a list of contacts which are known as connections and actively invite others to join your network and that whether they are existing LinkedIn users or not.

Now that you're a little more familiar with the LinkedIn community, let's go ahead and detail the numerous ways you can use LinkedIn to increase your business growth and get ahead of your competitors.

#1. Growing & Managing Your Contact List

Jeffrey Combs once said: "Your Networth Is Proportional To Your Network" and this statement is so true. In business, your contacts are everything. You don't know need to know everyone, but make sure you know the people that know everyone!

That being said, the LinkedIn community is a great place to begin connecting with real professionals in order to begin growing your list of business contacts which could be done pretty easily.

Just like any social networking site, you should approach like minded people to initiate the first contact (make sure that you're not spamming people with your ads) and regularly keep in touch with them so in the long run, they'll know, like and trust you.

In addition to this, you can import almost any digital address book and web email contacts (Hotmail, Aol, Yahoo, etc...) from your LinkedIn account hence growing your list of contacts.

#2. LinkedIn Answers

This tool is by far one of the most important tools on LinkedIn. "LinkedIn Answers" allow anyone to ask questions about any topic and anyone can answer these questions.

The cool thing about this is that you can interact with lots of people that are not in your network...Hence, a great way to increase your connections.

So Here's How It Works: When someone asks a question, everyone can give out answers or suggestions to that specific question.

A few days after the question has been posted and that you've received some answers, you'll be asked to choose the right answers or the answers that helped you most.

And out of all these good answers, you'll have to pick the "best" answer. Then the person that has been chosen for the "best" answer will be provided with an expertise point that will show up on his/her profile.

Answering questions is a great way to establish your expertise in a certain field. By answering more and more questions or inquiries from other LinkedIn users, you'll be able to gain more expertise points which will allow you to become the expert people are looking for to do business with.

Remember that in business, people join you or buy your products or services because you're an expert or a leader they know, like and trust.

With this little tool, you'll be able to drive a great deal of traffic to your site...Increasing sales and sign-ups!

You can easily become THAT expert in a really short period of time (anyone can become an expert in anything with just a simple research...Please do not share this secret with anyone!), hence attracting potential leads and prospects to your marketing funnels.

Asking questions is also a good way to interact with other experts. Your questions will be read and answered by so many people and you can make use of their expertise to do joint ventures or share business ideas.

#3. LinkedIn Services

The "LinkedIn Services" tool is a complete directory of service providers that have been recommended by other users in your network.

Let's say that you're looking for a highly qualified graphic & web designer in your town or city and you really want to make sure they're real experts. You can use the "LinkedIn Services" to see which graphic & web designers have been recommended by others.

This tool will help you save time researching for professionals you want to hire to get a certain job done.

That being said, I strongly suggest that you get your clients to recommend you as a professional so when people are searching for services or products you offer, then they'll find you.

That alone is priceless since you'll get tons of prospective clients at your fingertip without spending a penny on advertising.

#4. Search LinkedIn

The search tool simply allows you to find professionals that you know and even the ones you don't know.

Then you can either try to get an introduction from someone in your network that knows that person or simply upgrade your LinkedIn account in order to be able to contact him/her directly.

#5. LinkedIn Groups

LinkedIn groups allow you to join any group that you want. You'll then be able to meet great people and keep in touch with prospective business partners and clients.

Make sure that you're a contributing member of each group you join. Post great content regularly, keep in touch with the other group members, etc...This will literally help you brand your name, your products, services and even business opportunities because people will begin to relate to you.

#6. LinkedIn Jobs

LinkedIn is also a great place to post jobs or recruit employees to your company. Thousands of companies are hiring and recruiting on LinkedIn so if you're a business owner looking for prospective employees, there you go!

If you're looking for employment, there are so many great companies on LinkedIn offering great career opportunities.

#7. Search Engine Optimization Made Easy

SEO marketing is one the toughest things out there in cyberspace and takes a lot of effort and learning to become an expert.

Since LinkedIn is highly ranked in all top search engines, your LinkedIn page will easily show up in the top 10 in search engine results for certain keywords. That's literally free organic traffic your page without all the SEO marketing hassle.

Give it a try: simply type my name "Souleymane Maiga" on Google.com and on the 1st page, you'll see my LinkedIn profile.

#8. Conclusion

In conclusion, I would like to say that LinkedIn is a great social networking site. If used properly, it could increase your visibility and brand name.

It also adds more credibility to your image and brand ("LinkedIn Answers" easily allow you to become a known expert in your field of expertise).

Keep in mind that LinkedIn should not be used a mass marketing outlet like Facebook or MySpace or even Twitter (you should only target what you're looking forward to accomplish).